PLAN
OF THE
NAVY YARD
AT
...shington. D.C.

...osition and dimensions of all the buildings as

they were June 1st 1881

Scale 1inch = 100 Ft.

Officers' Quarters.

...nts Quarters A.
... B.
...structor's C.
...eer's D.

Commander's Quarters E.
Surgeon's "
Chief Engineer's " F.
Ordnance Officer's " H.
Marine Officer's " I & K.

Yard Buildings &c.

...nts Office.
...se and Office.
...way
...
...eer's Office.
... Bureau of Navigation.
...
...
...
...
...House.
...
...
Foundry
...achine Shop.
...dry
...
...ss.
...nt's Stables.
...rage Shop.
...House.
...ance Foundry
...hed
...Wheelwrights Shop.
...op with Blockmakers above.
...Shop.
...Shop.

42. Machine Shop with Pattern shop above.
43. Smithery.
44. Boilermakers Shop.
45. Cable Chains.
46. Forge Shop.
47. Anchor & Fagotting Shop
48. Boat House.
49. Boiler House. Ordnance Machine shop.
50. Ship "
51. Timber Shed with Mould & Sail Loft above
52. Scale 10 Tons.
53. Brass Foundry. Steam Engineering
54. Store House for Bureaus of Steam Engineering Construction, Repairs & Yards and Docks.
55. Fire Engine House.
56. Storehouse for Provisions & Clothing.
57. Iron Store & Ordinary, below Rigging Loft & Offices
58. Copper Rolling Mill.
59. Brass Foundry & Finishing Shops.
60. Cumboose & Tin Shop
61. Coppersmith Shop.
62. Paint Shop.
63. Shiphouse.
64. Prives.
65. Cranes.
66. Experimental Battery
67. Ammunition Store.
68. Office Experimental Battery.
69. Pendulum Gun for proving Powder.
70. Pitchhouse.
71. Coal Wharf.
72. Saluting Battery.
73. Masting Shears.
74. Watch Boxes.
75. Lamps.
76. Platform Scales 10 Tons.
77. Coal Shed
78. Bell.
79. Boilerhouse & large Chimney.
80. Flagstaff.
81. Store Equipment & Recruiting.
82. Gun Park.

... indicate Gaspipes.
... Drains.
... Waterpipes.
... Rail Track
... Steam Heating Pipes.

NAVY YARD
AT
Washington. D.C.

showing the position and dimensions of all the buildings as

they were June 1st 1881

Scale 1inch = 100 Ft.

Officers' Quarters.

Commandants Quarters A.
Captains " B.
Naval Constructor's " C.
Civil Engineer's " D.

Commander's Quarters E.
Surgeon's " F.
Chief Engineer's " G.
Ordnance Officer's " H.
Marine Officer's " I & K.

Yard Buildings &c.

1. Commandants Office.
2. Crane 65 Tons.
3. Guard House and Office.
4. Marine Railway.
5. Scales 75 Tons.
6. Dispensary.
7. Civil Engineer's Office.
8. Store House, Bureau of Navigation.
9. Ice House.
10. Museum
11. Fire Hydrant.
12. Ox stable.
13. Stables.
14. Woodshed.
15. Packing House.
16. Shed.
17. Fulminate House.
18. Mixing "
19. Finishing "
20. Rocket "
21. Cartilling "
22. Shell "
23. Timber Shed.
24. Laboratory.
25. Magazine.
26. Shed.
27. Ordnance Foundry.
28. " Machine Shop.
29. Iron Foundry.
30. Coal Sheds.
31. Rocket Press.
32. Acid House.
33. Commandant's Stables.
34. Gun Carriage Shop.
35. Sulphur House.
36. New Ordnance Foundry
37. Timber Shed.
38. Saw Mill Wheelwrights Shop.
39. Joiners Shop with Blockmakers above.
40. Erecting Shop.
41. Machine Shop.

42. Machine Shop with Pattern shop above.
43. Smithery.
44. Boilermakers Shop.
45. Cable Chains.
46. Forge Shop.
47. Anchor & Fagotting Shop.
48. Boat House.
49. Boiler House. Ordnance Machine shop.
50. Ship "
51. Timber Shed with Mould & Sail Loft above
52. Scale 10 Tons.
53. Brass Foundry. Steam Engineering
54. Store House for Bureaus of Steam Engineering Construction, Repairs & Yards and Docks.
55. Fire Engine House.
56. Storehouse for Provisions & Clothing.
57. Iron Store & Ordinary, below Rigging Loft & Offices.
58. Copper Rolling Mill.
59. Brass Foundry & Finishing Shops.
60. Cumboose & Tin Shop
61. Coppersmith Shop.
62. Paint Shop.
63. Shiphouse.
64. Prives.
65. Cranes.
66. Experimental Battery
67. Ammunition Store.
68. Office Experimental Battery.
69. Pendulum Gun for proving Powder.
70. Pitchhouse.
71. Coal Wharf.
72. Saluting Battery.
73. Masting Shears.
74. Watch Boxes.
75. Lamps.
76. Platform Scales 10 Tons.
77. Coal Shed.
78. Bell.
79. Boilerhouse & large Chimney.
80. Flagstaff.
81. Store Equipment & Recruiting.
82. Gun Park.

Note: Red Lines indicate Gaspipes.
Yellow " " Drains.
Blue " " Waterpipes.
Double black " Rail Track.
Dotted " Steam Heating Pipes.

Captain William Ramsey
United States Navy the
the dreadful let me come
they after ... Hand
they couldnt catch him a
prevails in alexandria
utmost that morning
theless the several pursue
way down to Richmond
as he ther and a state
a gentleman and a Soil
as greater one that
ther foot in the field
God allmighty about
wouldent let one
the federal constitution
mple under foot if he
ther as honest upright
ever lived he said no Res
personal while over they

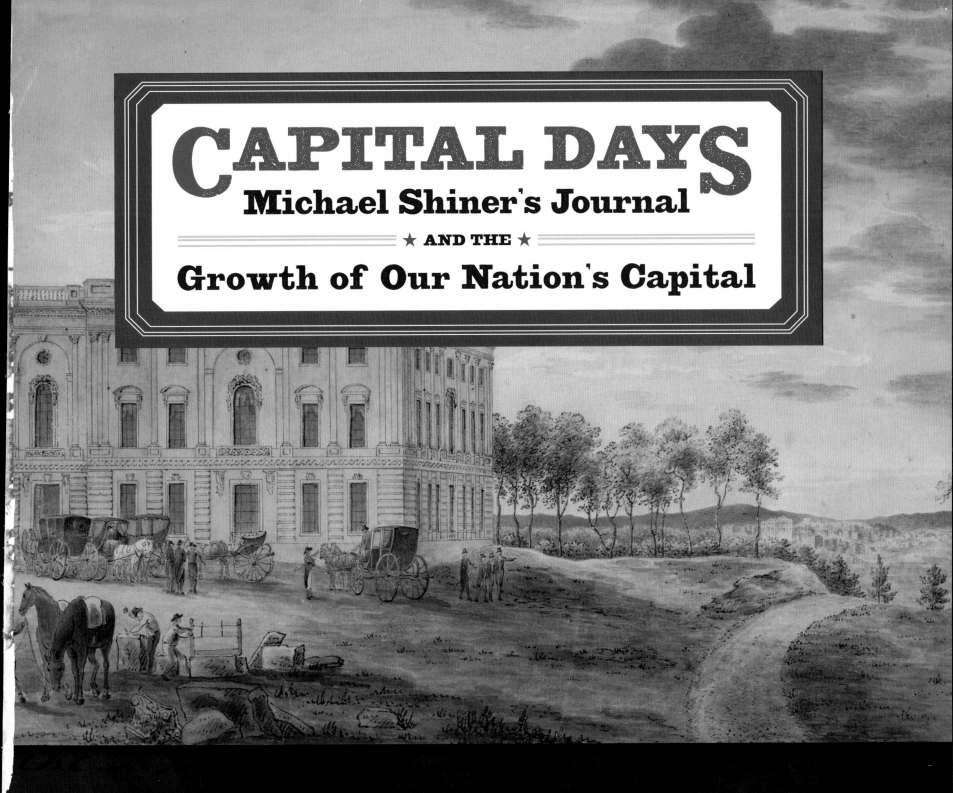

CAPITAL DAYS

Michael Shiner's Journal

★ AND THE ★

Growth of Our Nation's Capital

◈ TONYA BOLDEN ◈

ABRAMS BOOKS FOR YOUNG READERS

NEW YORK

Library of Congress Cataloging-in-Publication Data

Bolden, Tonya.
Capital days : Michael Shiner's journal and the growth of our nation's capital / by Tonya Bolden.
pages cm
Summary: "This book for young readers tells the story of Washington, D.C., through the story of an African American man, Michael Shiner, who lived there from approximately 1805 to 1880 and who kept a journal, excerpts of which are interspersed throughout the heavily illustrated text"— Provided by publisher.
Includes bibliographical references and index.
ISBN 978-1-4197-0733-9 (hardback)
1. Shiner, Michael, 1805–1880—Juvenile literature. 2. Shiner, Michael, 1805–1880—Diaries—Juvenile literature.
3. African Americans—Washington (D.C.)—Biography—Juvenile literature. 4. Freedmen—Washington (D.C.)—
Biography—Juvenile literature. 5. Slaves—Maryland—Biography—Juvenile literature. 6. Washington (D.C.)—
Biography—Juvenile literature. 7. Washington (D.C.)—History—19th century—Juvenile literature.
8. Washington (D.C.)—Race relations—History—19th century—Juvenile literature. I. Title.
F198.S54B65 2015
975.3'02092—dc23
[B]
2014024668

Text copyright © 2015 Tonya Bolden
For illustration credits, see page 85.
Book design by Pamela Notarantonio and Kate Fitch

The handwritten text used as background throughout the book is from page fifty-two of *Michael Shiner His Book.*

ENDPAPER (FRONT): *Plan of the Navy Yard at Washington, D.C., Showing the Position and Dimensions of All the Buildings As They Were June 1st 1881* (c. 1881), creator unknown.
ENDPAPER (BACK): *Map of the City of Washington, D.C.* (1851), by James Keily, surveyor.
TITLE PAGE: *A View of the Capitol,* detail (c. 1800), watercolor, by William Russell Birch.
FACING PAGE: *Plan of the City of Washington* (1798), published by J. Stockdale.

Printed and bound in China
10 9 8 7 6 5 4 3 2 1

Abrams Books for Young Readers are available at special discounts when purchased in quantity for premiums and promotions as well as fundraising or educational use. Special editions can also be created to specification. For details, contact
specialsales@abramsbooks.com or the address below.

ABRAMS

THE ART OF BOOKS SINCE 1949

115 West 18th Street
New York, NY 10011

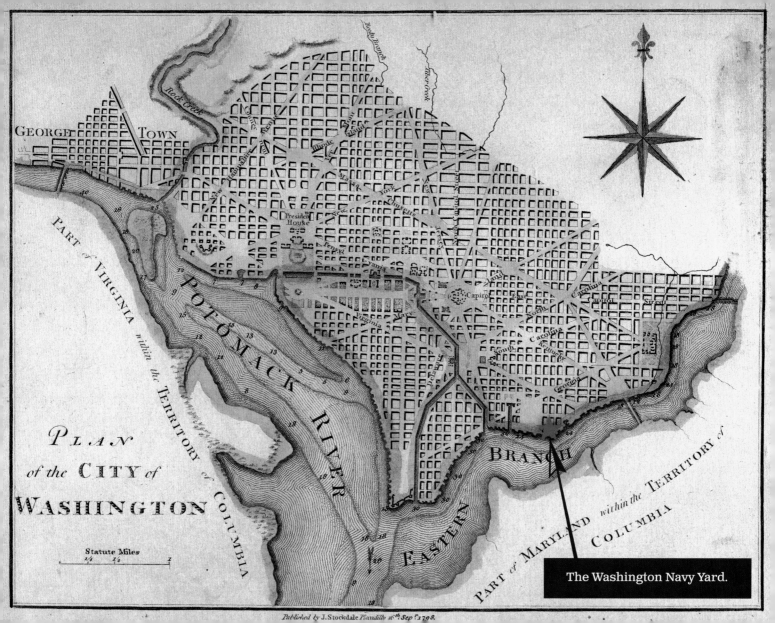

PLAN
of the CITY of
WASHINGTON

GEORGE TOWN

PART of VIRGINIA within the TERRITORY of COLUMBIA

POTOMACK RIVER

President House

Capitol

EASTERN BRANCH

PART of MARYLAND within the TERRITORY of COLUMBIA

The Washington Navy Yard.

Statute Miles

Published by J. Stockdale Piccadilly 16th Sept. 1798.

The City of Washington in 1800 (1804), a colored edition of an engraving by George Isham Parkyns. The view is from Virginia.

CONTENTS

A cluster of houses at the Navy Yard had been rapidly collected, but between . . . [Georgetown and the Navy Yard], Washington . . . lay in almost virgin nakedness. The grand avenue of Pennsylvania, running from one extreme to the other, had indeed been opened, as had also parts of other streets in the vicinity. The buildings in the city could then easily be counted. . . . Most of the area of the National Capital was then covered with bushes and undergrowth, which fell off here and there into pasture grounds and commons, or terminated in slashes and marshes.

—On America's capital in 1807, from *A Sketch of the Life of Dr. William Gunton*

1
"FLAMES OF FIRE"
★ AND ★
"ROCKETS'
RED GLARE"

The Black Boy (c. 1844), oil on canvas, by William Windus. Michael Shiner would have been about the age of this child during the War of 1812.

FLY! THAT'S WHAT ONE BOY ACHED TO DO WHEN Redcoats marched into the city, scaring him half to death. That boy was Maryland-born Michael Shiner, enslaved and about nine years old.

The place was the city of Washington, capital of a nation at war with Great Britain again, less than thirty years after the Revolution.

The stated causes were many. For one, Great Britain, in its long war with France, wanted the United States to stop trading with that nation, to deprive it of goods. So Great Britain tried to stymie that trade (by hijacking American merchant ships bound for France, for example). What's more, to feed the Royal Navy's need for sailors, British ships sometimes waylaid American ones and kidnapped their actual and supposed British-born crew members.

At root were ego and simmering enmity. Great Britain looked down its nose at the United States. The United States, its chest puffed out, would not be bullied. Too, it licked its lips over the prospect of seizing some of British North America, which included Upper and Lower Canada.

On June 1, 1812, President James Madison asked Congress for a declaration of war. He got it on June 18. Some would call the conflict that followed the Second War of Independence. Others, the War of 1812.

Early on, most of the combat was in the Great Lakes region and other places where U.S. and British territory touched (or nearly did). It was two years on when musket balls and bayonets came to Michael Shiner's world, as he so well remembered.

August 19, 1814: Several thousand British troops land at Benedict, Maryland, about forty miles south of the capital.

August 24, 1814: Yanks and Brits face off at the Battle of Bladensburg, about six miles northeast of the Capitol.

When the smoke cleared, the Americans were in flight. As British troops marched on the capital, scores of the scared fled. But not young Shiner, whose owner put him in the custody of a Mrs. Reid. She lived on Capitol Hill.

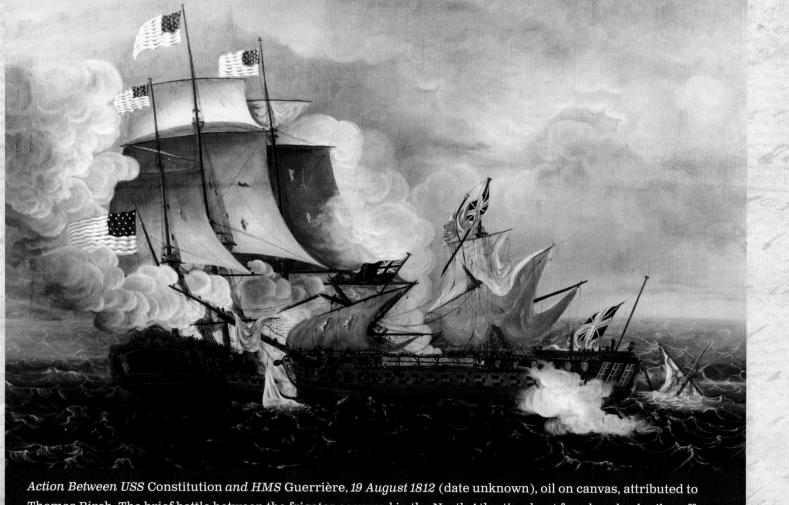

Action Between USS Constitution *and HMS* Guerrière, *19 August 1812* (date unknown), oil on canvas, attributed to Thomas Birch. The brief battle between the frigates occurred in the North Atlantic, about four hundred miles off the coast of Nova Scotia. The British ship is depicted striking her Union Jacks—that is, lowering her flags, a sign of surrender. The captain of the *Constitution* was Isaac Hull, someone Michael Shiner would come to know.

★ ★ ★

It was twilight when Redcoats marched along Pennsylvania Avenue and young Shiner heard "the tread of British army feet." To him, those soldiers were like "flames of fire—all red coats and the stocks of their guns painted with red vermillion and the iron work shined like a Spanish dollar." Shiner wanted to fly! But Mrs. Reid grabbed him. "Where are you running to, you nigger, you?" What a witch she was! "What do you reckon the British wants with such a nigger as you?" The terrified boy watched as the Redcoats marched on, "on towards the Capitol until they got against a large brick house on Capitol Hill."

That house belonged to Maryland planter Robert Sewall. When the Redcoats reached it, Robert Ross, one of their generals, had his horse shot out from under him. "In a twinkle of the eye," remembered Shiner, British troops surrounded the house, then "searched all through, upstairs and downstairs, in search of the man that shot the horse from under the general, but no man was found." Unable to punish the shooter, the British fired Congreve rockets at the house. "Those rockets burnt until they came to the explosion part. They made the rafters fly east and west."

Onward marched the Redcoats, intent on torching government buildings, especially the Capitol and the President's House.

The fires the British set burned into the next day, August 25, whereupon nature doused the flames—another day forever seared into Michael Shiner's memory: "I never shall forget that day one of the awful storms which raged for a long time without intermission. It thundered and lightninged, hailed and rained." What's more, a tornado hoisted "some ole houses up from off their foundations."

★ ★ ★

Capture of the City of Washington, a colored edition of an engraving published in volume 2 of *The History of England*, by Paul Rapin de Thoyras (1815).

After sacking the capital, the British aimed to take Baltimore, a prime port city and rich with privateers. Part of the plan was to seize its harbor guard, star-shaped Fort McHenry.

The attack began on September 13—bombs and rockets nonstop. Young Shiner, thirty miles south, "could hear the guns distantly."

Much closer was lawyer Francis Scott Key. Before the bombardment began and under a flag of truce, he boarded the British flagship to secure the release of an American physician taken prisoner of war.

Peering through early morning mist on September 14, Key was elated to see no symbol of British victory—no Union Jack flying atop the fort! Ecstatic, he scribbled down a poem about the Congreve rockets' red glare, bombs bursting in the air, and the broad stripes and bright stars of an American flag, still there.

★ ★ ★

A View of the Bombardment of Fort McHenry (c. 1816), a hand-colored edition of a c. 1814 aquatint by John Bower. The failed land invasion had started at North Point on September 12.

A VIEW of the BOMBARDMENT of Fort McHenry, near Baltimore, by the British fleet taken from the Observatory under the Command of Admirals Cochrane, & Cockburn, on the morning of the 13th of Sepr 1814 which lasted 24 hours, & thrown from 1500 to 1800 shells in the Night attempted to land by forcing a passage up the ferry branch but were repulsed with great loss.

Although fighting continued well into 1815, the War of 1812 was over on Christmas Eve, 1814. That's when U.S. and British representatives signed a treaty in the city of Ghent (in present-day Belgium). The peace boiled down to *status quo ante bellum*, Latin for "the state existing before the war": any land conquered would revert to the nation that had claimed it before the conflict. There had been some twenty thousand casualties during nearly three years of combat. Still, many Americans felt that the blood spilled, and the millions spent, had been worth it.

The British weren't likely to bully them anytime soon, they believed. The young U.S. Navy had given Great Britain's legendary Royal Navy several bloody noses.

★ ★ ★

As for America's capital, could it rise from the ashes? This marshy place that had already failed to live up to expectations?

Back in 1796, six years after the federal district had been established, William Thornton, architect of the original Capitol, assured a friend that Washington would be "the most splendid and beautiful city in

U.S. Capitol After Burning by the British (c. 1814), ink and watercolor on paper, by George Munger.

the world in a few years." That hadn't happened. Not enough people of pomp had moved there or put their money and prestige into making the city grand.

City? For many, calling the capital that was a stretch. "A meagre village" is what U.S. attorney general Richard Rush called it twelve days after the British invasion. "To a Bostonian or a Philadelphian," wrote Rush to former president John Adams,

"Washington appears like what it really is: a meagre village, a place with a few bad houses and extensive swamps, hanging upon the skirts too of a thinly peopled, weak, and barren country."

There was talk of moving the capital, but in the end hope prevailed that this "meagre village," in a diamond-shaped district measuring ten miles square, would one day indeed be a splendid and beautiful city.

And Michael Shiner would watch it grow.

CAPITAL DAYS
★TIMELINE★

APRIL 30, 1789: The inauguration of the first U.S. president, George Washington, a great hero of the American Revolution and a Virginia slaveholder. Location: Federal Hall in New York City, the nation's temporary capital.

JULY 16, 1790: President Washington signs the Residence Act. It establishes that the U.S. government's permanent seat will be in the South, along the Potomac River. This act also states that the federal district, which will be created out of land ceded by the slave states of Maryland and Virginia, is to be no larger than ten miles square (or 100 square miles).

JANUARY 24, 1791: President Washington announces the exact site of the federal district. Upon subsequent action by Congress, it would include the port towns of Georgetown (from Maryland) and Alexandria (from Virginia). Washington has selected Andrew Ellicott III of Maryland to survey the site. He in turn has chosen as one of his assistants a free black Marylander, Benjamin Banneker, an astronomer and mathematician.

MARCH 9, 1791: The man picked to design the capital, former Continental Army engineer Pierre Charles L'Enfant, arrives in Georgetown. In about a year, the temperamental Frenchman will be off the project. Ellicott will take L'Enfant's place.

We have agreed that the Federal District shall be called "The Territory of Columbia" and the Federal City "The City of Washington." The Title of the Map will therefore be, "A Map of the City of Washington in the Territory of Columbia."

We have also agreed the streets to be named alphabetically one way and numerically the other, the former divided into North and South Letters, the latter into East and West Numbers, from the Capitol.

—From a letter to Pierre Charles L'Enfant, September 9, 1791

The letter was from the commissioners overseeing the development of the seat of government: George Washington's friends Thomas Johnson, Daniel Carroll, and David Stuart. While "City of Washington" will stick, "District of Columbia" will soon replace "Territory of Columbia." (Miss Columbia, or Lady Columbia, is a goddess-like personification of the nation.)

OCTOBER 13, 1792: The cornerstone is laid in the city of Washington for the President's House, also known as the President's Palace, the Executive Mansion, and later the White House.

MARCH 4, 1793: The second inauguration of George Washington. Location: The Senate Chamber of Congress Hall in Philadelphia, the nation's temporary capital.

SEPTEMBER 18, 1793: The cornerstone for the Capitol is laid in the city of Washington.

MARCH 4, 1797: The inauguration of the second U.S. president, former vice president John Adams. Location: The House Chamber of Philadelphia's Congress Hall. Adams, never a slaveholder, was a native of Massachusetts, whose high court ruled slavery unconstitutional in 1783.

View of Blodget's Hotel in Washington, D.C. (c. 1799–1801), watercolor, by Nicholas King, a surveyor. The red-brick building on the hill far right (owned by Samuel Blodget Jr.) never really functioned as a hotel. For a time it housed a theater. When the War of 1812 broke out, it was home to several government offices, including the post office. This was the only significant government building in the capital not sacked and burned during the British invasion in 1814. Blodget's, known as Blodgett's, was where Congress first convened after the Capitol was torched.

OCTOBER 2, 1799: The Washington Navy Yard is established.

APRIL 24, 1800: President Adams signs off on the government spending $5,000 on "such books as may be necessary for the use of Congress."

MAY 15, 1800: President Adams directs federal departments to be open for business in the city of Washington by June 15.

JUNE 3, 1800: President Adams arrives in the federal district. He stays at a tavern in Georgetown, then at a hotel in Washington. He will not move into the President's House until November 1. First Lady Abigail Adams will arrive a few weeks later.

MARCH 4, 1801: The inauguration of the third U.S. president, Virginia slaveholder Thomas Jefferson, a former secretary of state (under Washington) and former vice president (under Adams). Location: A first-floor room in the Capitol (still under construction).

MAY 2, 1801: President Jefferson is notified that the 740 books for Congress's library, ordered in December 1800 from a London bookseller, have arrived. They will be housed in the Capitol.

1807: Three free black men who work at the Washington Navy Yard—George Bell (a carpenter) and Nicholas Franklin and Moses Liverpool (caulkers)—establish the first school for black children in the district. Named the Bell School, it will occupy a one-story wooden-frame building at Third and D Streets SE. The first teacher is a white man, Mr. Lowe. The founders of the Bell School, all born in slavery, are unable to read or write. The district's public school system, established in 1804, is for white children only.

MARCH 4, 1809: The inauguration of the fourth U.S. president, Virginia slaveholder James Madison, the "father of the Bill of Rights" and a former secretary of state (under Jefferson). Location: The Capitol's House Chamber (completed in 1807). That night, First Lady Dolley Madison hosts a fete at Long's Hotel: the first Inaugural Ball.

DECEMBER 31, 1810: The federal district has about 15,500 inhabitants. More than 10,000 are white. Of the blacks, 1,572 are free and 3,554 enslaved.

AUGUST 24–25, 1814: The burning of Washington.

───────────

James Smith, a free colored man who had accompanied [President] Madison to Bladensburg, galloped up to the house [about 3 p.m.], waving his hat, and cried out, "Clear out, clear out!" . . . All then was confusion. Mrs. Madison ordered her carriage, and passing through the dining-room, caught up what silver she could crowd into her old-fashioned reticule. . . .

[The British] did not arrive for some hours; in the mean time, a rabble, taking advantage of the confusion, ran all over the White House, and stole lots of silver and whatever they could lay their hands on.

About sundown I walked over to the Georgetown ferry, and found the President and all hands . . . waiting for the boat. It soon returned, and we all crossed over, and passed up the road about a mile; they then left us servants to wander about. . . . I [later] walked on to a Methodist minister's, and in the evening, while he was at prayer, I heard a tremendous explosion, and, rushing out, saw that the public buildings, navy yard, ropewalks, &c., were on fire.

—Paul Jennings

Jennings, fifteen when the British attacked the capital, was among the roughly one hundred people President Madison held in slavery and one of several working in the President's House (as opposed to on his plantation, Montpelier, in Virginia). Jennings had just set the dinner table when President Madison's messenger, James Smith, galloped up, sounding the alarm.

───────────

SEPTEMBER 19, 1814: Congress convenes at Blodgett's Hotel at Seventh and E Streets NW. Discussion begins about whether to rebuild the capital or move it (to Philadelphia, perhaps).

JANUARY 30, 1815: President James Madison approves the purchase of 6,487 volumes from former president Thomas Jefferson's personal library for the Congressional Library, which lost 3,000 volumes when the British burned the Capitol. The cost: $23,950. The works will be kept at first in Blodgett's Hotel, because that is still where Congress is meeting.

FEBRUARY 15, 1815: Congress approves the appropriation of $500,000 for the reconstruction of federal buildings in the capital.

JULY 4, 1815: The cornerstone is laid for a three-story brick building on First Street NE. It will serve as Congress's temporary home while the Capitol is restored. The U.S. Supreme Court's building will one day rise on the site of this brick building.

DECEMBER 13, 1815: Congress convenes in "the Old Brick Capitol" for the first time.

I confess that I was so unfeminine as to be free from fear, and willing to remain in the Castle [President's House]. If I could have had a cannon through every window, but alas! those who should have placed them there fled before me, and my whole heart mourned for my country! I remained nearly three days out of town, but I cannot tell you what I felt on re-entering—such destruction—such confusion!

—First Lady Dolley Madison, December 3, 1814

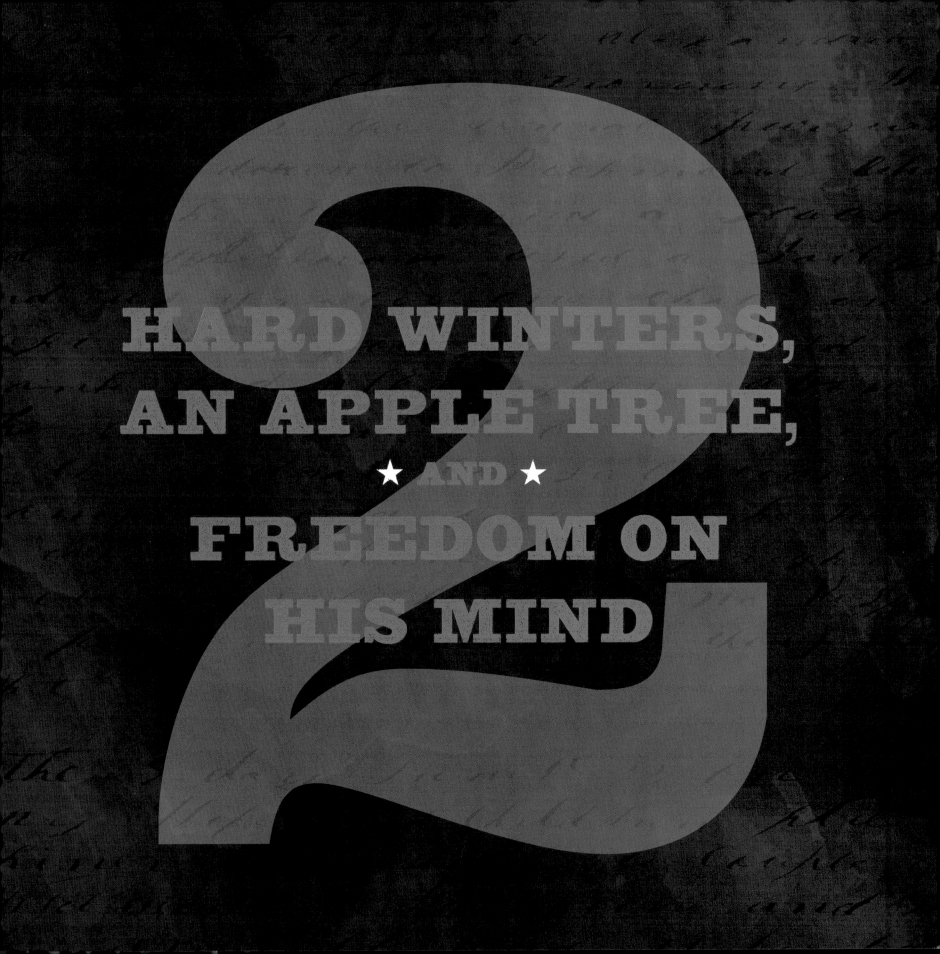

1813

ther was a Horse Company organised in this City of Washington By Captin lower Caudwell Docter Edward Clerk Belong to it and James Freind Formly a Raker on the Hill thosmas renols formly a tarvan keper at the eastern Branch Bridge on pensylvana avenu James kely formly kept a redervus on the navy yard hill a Raker useto Belong to this company By the name of Burns formly use to Have a Bake hose South of the long row and a Brother in law of lower Giorge Water stone all those a Bove name id gintelman use to Belong to that Company organise in 1813 By Captin thomas Carkey a young man By the name of spunangle his Father and John Conon was a Black smith formly kept a Black smith shop south of the congress Burial groun rigments of infertry By Captin thomas Carkey ther was a company of peild artilry organnised at the same time By capten Samuel Burch and thomas Howard and thomas Warfield and louyd pumphrey and Joseph Brow police of the 5 Ward Isaac philips Belonge to it his Mother formly the shop Below the captol all those named gentlemen use to Belonge too

ia Company organnised By mos Huse formly kept a on pensylvania avenu ner the Centre Market elisha pumphery uto Belong to it John Moody use to Belonge to it

Page 1 of *Michael Shiner His Book*, with memories of the capital's early volunteer firefighting companies and military units, which included members of the Pumphrey family.

restoring the capital labored during hard times. "Ice commenced early in November 1814 and it continued freezing until the middle of March 1815." So remembered Michael Shiner.

"And 1816 was a hard winter." Young Shiner saw "three black spots in the sun" and, at winter's end, a sun "as red as blood." Then came "a frost every night [and] the whole summer there was no corn. . . . It was all withered up."

It wasn't only in Shiner's world that people saw sunspots and scary suns and suffered weird weather. This was "the Year Without Summer." Its cause lay in a disaster that struck the island of Sumbawa, in present-day Indonesia. In April 1815, Mount Tambora blew. It was the largest volcanic eruption in recorded history.

Tens of thousands of islanders died in the cataclysm. So did fish, fowl, and other life-forms. The clouds of ash drifted far and wide, blocking the sun's rays and causing a big chill around the globe.

Winter in June!—During the past week the weather has been extremely cold for the season and we have experienced several severe frosts, which have nearly destroyed the gardens and done much injury to the crops of grain. On Thursday morning a considerable quantity of SNOW fell. . . .
—Geneva Gaz. of June 12.

—*New York Courier*, June 18, 1816

The *Geneva Gazette* was a newspaper in upstate New York.

The War of 1812, hard winters, and corn all withered up are near the start of Michael Shiner's memories, scribbled in a workaday notebook. The result was a memoir of sorts, composed when he was up in age and structured as a diary, a log, a daybook, a journal. Its title, simple and blunt: *Michael Shiner His Book.*

Michael Shiner His Book leaves many aspects of its author's life in shadow and mystery. Shiner never named his parents, never wrote about sisters or brothers. Whatever his broodings, his musings on slavery, Shiner kept those to himself. Pen pictures of his personal life come in fits and starts, flare up, then fade away. It was America's life, especially its capital, that Shiner was keen on chronicling, from events that made headline news to those the press would never find newsworthy. Things like: "One cedar tree planted in Washington Navy Yard. One apple tree planted by Michael Shiner in front of the boatswain's house on the 17th day of March 1827 (a Saturday)."

"Those trees will not live," said the boatswain, David Eaton.

The still-enslaved Michael Shiner was no longer a scared little boy who could be stopped in his tracks by the likes of nasty Mrs. Reid. Shiner came through the war and other woes quite a bold soul, seemingly fearless. Now about age twenty-two, he stood up for those saplings. "Sir," he replied, "those trees will be here when you and me are dead and gone."

Those were Shiner's last words about the cedar and apple trees but not about the Washington Navy Yard, about a mile east of the Capitol, on the banks of the Eastern Branch, as the Anacostia River was called. The Washington Navy Yard is where Shiner had been put to work as a teen. To toil sometimes twelve hours a day, six days a week, to see his earnings go to his owner. That was William Pumphrey Jr. of Piscataway, Maryland, where Shiner was likely born. Pumphrey was among the scores of slaveholders in and around the capital who, before and after the War of 1812, leased black people to construction crews working on the President's House, the Capitol, and other buildings and who rented them out to the Yard. And that's where Shiner continued to work after he was sold on September 8, 1828. The price: $250.

Shiner's new owner was Thomas Howard Sr., chief clerk of the Yard. He lived on the corner of Third and N Streets SE, a few blocks from the U.S. Navy's first home port and the nation's number-one shipyard early on. Its mission changed in the fall of 1827, when the Board of Naval Commissioners decided that the Yard should be a major

List of Slaves, who are conceived necessary to retain viz:

Names	To whom belonging	How employed in the Yard
Joe Byus	Captⁿ Jnᵒ Davidson of Wash	Striker in the Smiths shop
Jim Brown	Thos Murray master cooper	Ditto
Luke Cannon	Mr Fenwick Dist Colum	Ditto
Joe Edwards	David Dobbin Orarian Yᵈ (hired)	Ditto
Basill Nevitt	Widow Nevitt of Washt	Ditto
Joe Smoot	Alexr Smoot Dᵒ	Ditto
Joe Thompson	Walter Clark Dᵒ	Ditto
Antᵒ Washington ⎱ Widow Sarah Washington Dᵒ		Ditto
Chas Washington ⎰		
Davy Bean	George Bean Dᵒ	Blower in Smiths shop
Lech Nally	Rebecca Nally Dᵒ	Ditto
Pompey Slate	Alexr Smoot Dᵒ	Ditto
Bill Barnes	Thos Howard Ovr Yᵈ (hired)	Carpenters laborer & borer
Bill Campbell	Mr Fenwick Dist Colum	Ditto dᵒ
Harry Hicks	Mr Evans of Wash	Ditto dᵒ
Roger Howard	Thos Howard Navy Yard	Ditto dᵒ
Luke Rivers	Michl Lowe of Washt	Ditto dᵒ
Zeph Woodland	Jmº Caldwell Dᵒ	Ditto dᵒ
Bill Holmes	Joseph Cassin Dᵒ	Pitch boiler
Harry Smallwood ⎱ Widow Linda Smallwood Dᵒ		Turns Grindstones
Heziah Smallwood ⎰		
Peter Selby	Philip Selby Dᵒ	Caulkers warmer
Bill Hamilton	Francis Hamilton Dᵒ	Dᵒ Ditto

Navy Yard Washtn 12 May 1808

Ths Tingey

supplier of "blocks, chain cables, anchors, castings, cambooses, brass work, chain pumps, lanterns, hand arms, rockets, etc."

Michael Shiner worked in the Yard's Ordinary—the department in charge of ships not in use but still in need of upkeep and, often, repairs. "Ordinary" men didn't just tend to the ships. They cleared snow, dug holes, loaded carts. They hauled stuff, too: timber to sheds, tin from the cooper's shop to the sailing loft, coils of rigging from the rigging loft, bricks and sand to construction sites. But landlubbers they were not.

"Up oars, my lads, shove off, let fall, give way!" commanded coxswain John Green. This navigator was giving the let's-go to Michael Shiner, Basil Brown, and four other enslaved men rowing Yard commandant Thomas Tingey's gig. This was back on the Fourth of July 1828.

On that fine Friday morning, graced with flying clouds and an easy breeze, the black crew, all in full-dress sailor uniforms, took Tingey down the Eastern Branch, then up the Potomac to Georgetown. The commandant had a rendezvous with President John Quincy Adams.

In Georgetown, Shiner watched the president make his way to the wharf with other bigwigs, then board the *Surprise*, a steamboat that had traveled with Tingey's gig. Both boats were soon off to Little Falls, Maryland, where President Adams, age sixty, proved himself more than up to the task of digging a hole, the symbolic start of a construction project—witnessed, remembered Shiner, by "great masses of people" treated to "plenty of everything to eat and drink."

Shiner was impressed when Adams "pulled off his coat and took hold of the spade as if he was going to set in for a day's work and went right into it! And that was the beginning of the Chesapeake and Ohio Canal." Later that day in his diary, Adams explained why he had flung off his coat: "It happened that at the first stroke of the spade, it met immediately under the surface a large stump of a tree. After repeating the stroke three or four times without making any impression, I threw off my coat and, resuming the spade, raised a shovel full of the earth, at which a general shout burst forth from the surrounding multitude."

When completed in 1850, the 185-mile C&O Canal would be a boon to people (such as farmers) and firms (such as coal companies) moving goods between Cumberland, Maryland, and Georgetown.

★ ★ ★

Back at the Yard after the C&O Canal groundbreaking, Shiner and his mates got a pass—permission to leave. Off they went to Capitol Hill, where they got truly "spirited" at a tavern run by a black man, George Lee. Shiner described Lee as "formerly a slave to old Mr. Watterston and set free by Mr. Watterston, the father of lawyer George Watterston." "Old Mr. Watterston"—David—was a master builder from Scotland who had worked on the Capitol. His son George was the third chief of the Congressional Library.

Shiner didn't say how George Lee came to have his own business. He only mentioned the names of the alcoholic drinks Lee served, such as "Spark Fire," "the Run from the Gun," and "Didn't Know Where You Were." Sadly, Shiner drank far too much. When he wandered back to the Yard the next morning, he was in a mean mood.

"Are you a drunken sailor?" quipped a young black man.

Shiner went berserk! "I seized hold of

the fellow and we had a small tussle for a while and I threw the fellow into the mud hole. Then I staggered off about my business and went in the Yard."

There, Shiner got into another scrape with another black man, Sam Reid, Commandant Tingey's coachman. After the sentry broke up that fight, he reported Shiner to the first lieutenant of the Yard, John Kelly, a nephew of Tingey's and also a slaveholder.

Shiner wasn't the only one in the soup. The commandant's footman, also enslaved, had been "cutting some of his shines." Definitely not a good move, for Tingey had a vicious turn of mind. (In an ad he placed in 1821 about the escape of Sukey, one of his domestic workers, Tingey declared, "If her tongue could be safely extracted she would be a most excellent servant.")

For his mischief, Tingey's footman got a "starting"—a beating with a boatswain's starter, a rope whip used to keep sailors on their toes. "And they were going to give me a starting, too," recalled Shiner, adding that he didn't get whipped after all. For that, he thanked three men. One was Lieutenant Kelly.

What moved Kelly and the others to save Shiner's skin was probably regard for his owner, Thomas Howard, who had power. As

Captain Thomas Tingey (1869), oil on canvas, by Orlando S. Lagman, after John Trumbull. Tingey, a former member of the British Royal Navy, joined the U.S. Navy in 1798, a year before the Washington Navy Yard was established. It was Tingey who got the Yard up and running—from the first wharf to the first ships built. When the British attacked the capital in August 1814, Tingey ordered the Navy Yard burned, with permission from superiors. They preferred to see it in ashes than in British hands.

Shiner scholar John G. Sharp explains, Howard "often acted for the Commandant in business and administrative matters." What's more, the chief clerk "had charge of the civilian musters and payrolls. Consequently, he was the 'go-to-guy' for getting someone a job."

Shiner recounted only once of Howard striking him. Apparently, the chief clerk wasn't big on violence, something Kelly and others at the Yard would have known. But Shiner's deliverance from a starting wasn't enough to make him meek and mild. He would again drink and become disorderly—and he wasn't alone in that. Drunkenness was common in the capital. As journalist Jefferson Morley put it, the city's many taverns and grog shops made it a place where "one could easily get drunk."

Disorder wasn't rare, either. Fights even happened in places where people ought to have been on their best behavior—like the Capitol. There, lawmakers had fistfights and cane fights. Many packed pistols. And it's where President John Quincy Adams's son and private secretary, John Adams II, was attacked in mid-April 1828. He was in the Capitol Rotunda, on his way to deliver a message to the Senate Chamber, when newspaperman Russell Jarvis pounced on him, reportedly pulling his nose. It was payback for an insult at a recent reception at the President's House. Bystanders broke up the ensuing scuffle and the incident soon blew over, but it amplified the need for the Capitol to have more than four watchmen. Before the month was out, Congress had created the U.S. Capitol Police.

Months later, on Christmas Eve, Michael Shiner was again feeling his oats. Having gotten a pass, and with "Christmas in me," he was looking forward to visiting friends in Piscataway, about fifteen miles south of the capital. He hadn't gone far when a pack of boys surrounded him. They had sport on their minds and firecrackers in their hands. "And you may depend on it," Shiner recalled. "They lit me up torchlight fashion for a while with the firecrackers."

A white man singled out Shiner for rebuke. "You scamp, what are you doing here?" he asked, striking him. Shiner hit the man back—unaware he was a justice of the peace. The next thing Shiner knew, the firecracker crew had chased him to Smack Alley, but he staved them off and stayed there until his owner came.

"Mike, you scamp, what's the matter with you?" scolded Thomas Howard.

Back at the Yard, Shiner kicked up a ruckus, was tossed in the guardhouse, and then was put in "double irons, hand and foot." But it could have been worse. By law, for hitting any white man, let alone a justice of the peace, Shiner could have had an ear cropped—that is, had all or part of it cut off. Again, he'd caught a break. He also wasn't locked up for long.

On Christmas Day, remembered Shiner, "between 4 and 5 o'clock in the morning Master Tommy came and took me out and carried me down home." Howard gave Shiner breakfast and some money, as well as a hard charge before letting him go on his way: "Behave yourself and don't drink any more whisky!"

Michael Shiner did not obey. He wound up in a tavern in Piscataway, and later kicked up his heels at a party on a farm. "I never enjoyed myself better in all my life. We danced all night!"

On his way home the next day, Shiner found himself in an awful fix again. He was halfway home, on Fort Washington's wharf, when soldiers meddled with him. One asked whence he hailed, calling him "Jack," short for *Jack-tar*, slang for *sailor*. And that was apt. Shiner was dressed like a sailor: blue frock shirt, blue trousers, blue roundabout jacket, red vest, tarpaulin hat.

Shiner told the soldiers he was from the Washington Navy Yard. They pegged him instead as a runaway from the *St. Louis*, a sloop that had recently set sail to join the Pacific Squadron in patrolling waters where pirates were prone to pounce on American merchant ships. It wasn't unreasonable for someone to think Shiner might have been a member of the *St. Louis*'s crew. Though blacks were officially banned from serving in the U.S. armed forces after the Revolution, the Navy took all the black men (and boys) it could get, free and enslaved, because of constant manpower shortages.

Shiner didn't have his pass to prove he was telling the truth—he'd given it to the sentry as he left the Yard, per protocol. But even if he'd had a pass, it might not have mattered. Blacks, whatever their legal status, lived in fear of being kidnapped and sent into slavery in the Deep South, with its growing number of labor-intensive rice, cane, and cotton plantations.

The temptation to kidnap blacks and sell them to slave dealers was high. The city of Washington was the Upper South's capital of the domestic slave trade. Before being led in coffles through the city streets to ships heading farther south, children and adults—some kidnapped, others coldly sold by their owners—endured hellish days and nights in private jails commonly called "slave pens." The capital had several of these jails.

One day I went to see the "slaves' pen"... about half a mile [from the Capitol].... It is surrounded by a wooden paling fourteen or fifteen feet in height, with the posts outside to prevent escape, and separated from the building by a space too narrow to admit of a free circulation of air. At a small window above, which was unglazed and exposed alike to the heat of summer and the cold of winter... two or three sable faces appeared, looking out wistfully to while away the time and catch a refreshing breeze; the weather

being extremely hot. In this wretched hovel, all colors, except white—the only guilty one—both sexes, and all ages, are confined.... some of them, if my informants are to be believed, having been actually frozen to death, during the inclement winters which often prevail in the country.

—Edward Strutt Abdy

Abdy was a white Englishman who toured America from April 1833 to October 1834. The jail he visited was in Washington Robey's tavern at Seventh Street and Maryland Avenue SW.

Michael Shiner wasn't taking any chances with those soldiers. Try as they did to detain him—"I had a terrible affray with them on the wharf"—he got free, then finally back to the capital. Once there, acting as if he were master of himself, Shiner didn't head straight to the Yard, where he was due. Instead, he dropped in on a white ship's carpenter, Jesse Morrison. He lived on Navy Yard Hill, the settlement that grew up around the shipyard.

Saturday, December 27th 1828
This day light variable winds and fair weather.... Ordinary men clearing about the officers dwellings. Michl Shiner who had

Kidnapping, engraving, by Alexander Rider, from *A Portraiture of Domestic Slavery in the United States* (1817), by Jesse Torrey. This drawing illustrates a free woman's kidnapping in the capital. The book's author, a white abolitionist and Philadelphia physician, interviewed the woman after she regained her liberty.

liberty out from Wednesday till Friday morning has not came in yet.

—Washington Navy Yard log

For returning late on December 28, Shiner paid a price. No more passes for him until January 25. But before January was out, it wasn't his liberty that was in jeopardy but his life.

★ ★ ★

On Thursday, January 29, 1829, with ice "just a-breaking up in the river," Shiner was among the three or four Ordinary men rowing a jolly boat sent to Alexandria for supplies. These included a half barrel of pilot bread.

"Mike, take that barrel and carry it forward so as to give yourselves room to row." So said the man at the helm, rigger James Smith, as the jolly boat was returning to the Yard. As Shiner followed orders, the barrel hoops slipped off—"and overboard I went."

Shiner struggled for his life in the icy water. He went down once, twice, and then

Mate John Thompson caught hold of him. "Nine Lives" Shiner lived to see another day.

One of those days was Friday, February 20, 1829, when a fire broke out a few blocks from the Yard in the Marine Barracks, the corps' headquarters. It consumed the center building, despite the valiant efforts of Shiner and others: "We went out to the fire at that time a little before the bell rang for twelve and we stayed at the garrison until between 1 and 2 o'clock in the night—and the coldest night I ever felt in my life. . . . It was so cold that the hose freezed up. They formed lines in different sections, passed the water with buckets to the fire. And they worked like men."

And there was Monday, February 23, 1829, the day Commandant Thomas Tingey died.

Saturday, April 11, 1829, the day Commodore Isaac Hull took Tingey's place.

And Monday, May 11, 1830, the day boatswain David Eaton got a whack "right across the small of the back" when another worker lost his grip on a pair of log tongs.

Scarier was Saturday, February 12, 1831: the day of a solar eclipse. "It lasted from half past 11 o'clock until half past 3 o'clock. It was so dark at dinner hour . . . that we had to light the candles to see how to eat."

Another enslaved man, Nat Turner, reportedly saw the eclipse as a sign from God to move from rage to violent rebellion against slavery. Months later, in August 1831, Turner led a revolt in and around the town of Jerusalem, in Southampton County, Virginia. Blacks killed roughly sixty whites, including

City of Washington from Beyond the Navy Yard (1833), oil on canvas, by George Cooke. To the left of the schooner is the multi-windowed ship house, where ships were stored and keels were built. To the right of the schooner is the cavernous boat house, where big gunboats were built. Shiner spent a great deal of time in these buildings—and trudging to and from them. Just as he watched the capital grow up, so he watched the Washington Navy Yard do the same.

read and write. (Nat Turner had been literate.) Despite all this, blacks kept planning rebellions, from escapes to learning to read and write. The only acts of black rebellion Michael Shiner wrote about were his own. Of course, drinking and brawling didn't help his plight. And that hung in the balance on December 4, 1832, the day his owner, Thomas Howard, died.

★ ★ ★

At the time, America was reeling from an outbreak of cholera, a disease usually contracted by consuming contaminated food or water. "It raged in the City of Washington," remembered Michael Shiner, "and every day there were twelve or thirteen carried out to their graves . . . and that was a small number to what died in different parts of the country a day."

It wasn't cholera that killed Thomas Howard at the age of fifty-four, but rather consumption.

children. In the aftermath, Nat Turner and many of his followers were hanged.

Michael Shiner His Book is silent on Nat Turner, and silent on the South's backlash against blacks after the uprising. In Southampton, scores who had nothing to do with Turner's revolt, including children, were beaten, maimed, and killed. Virginia soon made it illegal to teach any blacks to

Shiner recorded Howard's death in his book but not the anxiety he surely felt. Slaveholders sometimes freed people outright in their wills. Sometimes they ordered them to be sold, causing great agony and hard wondering: *Will I wind up with somebody near or far? Will my new master be somewhat merciful or a brute?* Death was how Shiner had gone from being William Pumphrey Jr.'s property to being Thomas Howard's.

In his will of August 12, 1827, Pumphrey had mandated that the eight people he held in slavery be sold to pay his debts—sold not as slaves for life but as "term" slaves. The youngest, Charlotte, about the age of two, was to serve another twenty-six years in bondage, whereas Michael Shiner, about twenty-two, was to serve another fifteen.

Some slaveholders saw term slavery as a way to maximize their investment. They reasoned that if people in bondage knew they would one day be freed, they would be less likely to attempt escape and more likely to be diligent workers (no slowdowns, no sabotage). Also, if slaveholders freed people before they reached middle age, they wouldn't have to feed, clothe, and house them when they were unable to work as hard as they once had. Other slaveholders opted for term slavery because they couldn't abide the idea of claiming lifetime ownership of other human beings.

When Thomas Howard bought Shiner in 1828, he agreed to the terms in Pumphrey's will. What's more, Howard promised to reduce Shiner's sentence of servitude by about half. But Michael Shiner couldn't be sure of anything until Howard's will was probated—that is, proved valid. That happened on December 21, 1832, about two weeks after his death.

Thomas Howard left everything he owned to his wife, Ann Nancy, from his real estate to his "Negroes": a Maria and her two children, a Louisa, a John, and, yes, Michael Shiner. However, there was at least a "but" when it came to him.

"But having purchased a Negro Man named Michael Shiner for the term of fifteen years only, and having promised to manumit and set him free at the expiration of eight years, if he conducted himself worthy of such a privilege, it is my will and desire and I hereby set free and manumit the said Michael Shiner, at the expiration of eight years from the date of said purchase."

If Howard's will were honored, Michael Shiner would have his liberty in 1836. Four years—that's how long he would have to wait while he cleared snow from the Yard, loaded carts, hauled tin and timber and rigging, and rowed a jolly boat.

★ ★ ★

When Thomas Howard died, Shiner's own freedom couldn't have been the only freedom on his mind. He had a wife and children, and they, too, were in slavery. The family had been allowed to live together somewhere near or in the Yard. The exact location is unknown; Shiner was mum about his family life in his book, and enslaved people weren't listed in city directories.

How Shiner's wife, Phillis, wound up in the capital is not a mystery. Back in October 1817, James Pumphrey, a brother of Shiner's former owner, had filed a slave certificate for her with the court. In it, he stated that he brought Phillis from Loudoun County, Virginia, to the capital for his own use "and not for sale."

Phillis was about nine years old at the time. Michael was about twelve. Like

The third and last page of a "List of the Goods Belonging to the Personal Estate of Thomas Howard (deceased)," certified and witnessed on January 8, 1833, about a month after the chief clerk of the Washington Navy Yard died. Along with barrels, baskets, a cow, and other possessions, we find people, including one "Black Man M. Shiner Slave for four [more] years" valued at $100.

Howard, James Pumphrey lived in Ward Five, so Phillis and Michael may have become friends as children, then sweethearts as teens. When Howard died in late 1832, the Shiners had two little girls, Ann and Harriet. There was a baby on the way, too: a girl they'd name Mary Ann. By law, whoever owned an enslaved woman also owned her children (whether the father was enslaved or free, and no matter what his race or ethnicity).

With his family's fate in the hands of James Pumphrey, Michael Shiner must have been in a world of worry when, several months before Thomas Howard died, James Pumphrey breathed his last breath. Because Pumphrey died in debt, Michael Shiner's wife and children were put up for sale, along with a bedstead and bedding, hammers and a hatchet, flatware, stoneware, a coffee mill, a sidesaddle, a bay mare, tables, chairs, kettles, and more. The family was bought for $295 by a local man: James Pumphrey's son Levi. But they didn't stay his for long.

"The 5th day of June 1833 (a Wednesday) my wife and children . . . were sold to . . . Mr. Franklin and Mr. John Armfield, and were carried down to Alexandria on the sixth day of June 1833 (a Thursday)." Shiner's family had been "snatched away" from him between Seventh and Eighth Streets near West Alley.

The men who now possessed Shiner's wife and daughters operated what was then America's largest slave-dealing firm. Through responses to their ads and by other means, Isaac Franklin and John Armfield purchased about a thousand people a year in the district, Maryland, and Virginia. They resold most of them to planters in the Deep South.

When Michael Shiner discovered that his family was gone, he was in agony and intent on getting them back! "The 7th of June 1833 (a Friday) I went to Alexandria three times in one day over the Long Bridge and I was in great distress."

Were tears streaming down his face as he made those trips—about twelve miles each way?

Was he spitting, cussing mad?

Silently frantic?

He didn't say. He only told of the outcome: "With the assistance of God, I got my wife and children clear."

FRANKLIN & ARMFIELD'S SLAVE PRISON.

This establishment is in Alexandria. It is a handsome three story brick house, neatly painted, with green blinds, and the sign, FRANKLIN & ARMFIELD over the door. It has attached to it a large yard, perhaps 300 feet square, enclosed by a high close board fence neatly white-washed, and filled with various small buildings. Mr. Leavitt visited it in 1834. One of the partners lives in New-Orleans, and the other in Alexandria. The latter, says Mr. L. "politely invited us to go and see the Slaves. We were first taken out into a paved yard, 40 or 50 feet square, with a very high brick wall and about half of it covered with a roof. This yard is appropriated to the men. He ordered the men to be called out from the cellar where they sleep, and they soon came up, to the number of 50 or 60, and ranged themselves irregularly before us. While they were standing, he ordered the girls to be called out, when the door opened, and about 50 women and small children came in. They were all clothed decently in coarse but apparently comfortable garments. Some three or four had children, so young that they brought them in their arms; and I thought I saw in the faces of *these mothers* some indications of irrepressible feeling. It seemed to me that they hugged their little ones more closely, and that a cold perspiration stood on their foreheads, and I thought I saw tears too. There were in all about 28 children under 10 years of age."

The standing advertisement of this house in the Washington papers is as follows:—

"CASH FOR 400 NEGROES."

"Including both sexes, from 12 to 25 years of age. Persons having likely servants to dispose of, will find it to their interest to give us a call, as we will give higher prices in cash than any other purchaser who is now, or may hereafter come into this market."

"FRANKLIN & ARMFIELD."

Draw at Longbridge [sic], *Washington City* (1839), a wash drawing, by Augustus Köllner. This toll bridge—built in 1809, burned during the War of 1812, and subsequently rebuilt and upgraded over the years—is now part of the the Fourteenth Street Bridge complex.

Shiner was eternally grateful to several people. Boatswain David Eaton was one. Commandant Isaac Hull was another. There was also Major General Hamlin. He got Phillis and the girls out of Franklin and Armfield's jail and into Alexandria's county jail on June 7, pending further action. That action came four days later. Not only would Shiner's family soon be out of the county jail, but on that day they would be out of slavery—freed!

Their freedom decree began: "Know all men by these presents that I, Levi Pumphrey, of the City of Washington in the District of Columbia, for divers good and sufficient causes me thereunto moving have manumitted, emancipated, set free and released from slavery a negro woman named Phillis and her three children named Ann, Harriet, and Mary Ann purchased by me at a sale of my father's property." Pumphrey reckoned Shiner's wife about age twenty-five and his daughters about four years, three years, and four months old.

The causes "moving" Levi Pumphrey to void the sale to Franklin and Armfield and then to free Shiner's family? Most certainly there was pressure and also cash raised by white men who came to Shiner's aid. Chances are, the cash was money that Shiner vowed to pay back, perhaps with his labor, perhaps with a portion of the earnings the late chief clerk's widow let him have. Too, Shiner may have been doing work on the side, such as whitewashing fences or chopping firewood.

It must have been pressure and money motivating Levi Pumphrey. The man hadn't suddenly become righteous. His slaveholding continued for years, evidenced by an ad that ran in the *Daily National Intelligencer* twenty-five years later, in September 1858. It offered a hundred-dollar reward for each of two men who had escaped from him, Hanson and Gusta. Both were interviewed by William Still of Philadelphia, a top agent on the Underground Railroad and its finest record keeper. In that interview Hanson described Levi Pumphrey as "a perfect savage."

Be that as it may, back in the summer of 1833, what mattered to Michael Shiner was that his wife and children had their liberty—and he hoped to be free, too, in three years. How they must have rejoiced once home together again.

Perhaps they danced all night!

CAPITAL DAYS
★TIMELINE★

All of the quotations that appear below and in the other timelines are from *Michael Shiner His Book*, unless indicated otherwise in the Notes section that begins on page 77.

MARCH 4, 1817: The inauguration of the fifth U.S. president, James Monroe, a former secretary of state and secretary of war (both under Madison) and a Virginia slaveholder. Location: Outside the Old Brick Capitol.

JANUARY 1, 1818: President Monroe and First Lady Elizabeth Monroe host a grand reopening of the restored President's House.

DECEMBER 6, 1819: The start of the first session of the Sixteenth U.S. Congress and the day on which its members first meet in the Capitol's restored House and Senate chambers. The Capitol's center section is still under construction.

MARCH 6, 1820: President Monroe signs the Missouri Compromise, Maine enters the Union as a free state, Missouri as a slave state. As for the rest of the Louisiana Purchase, out of which Missouri was created, slavery is banned north of the parallel 36°30'.

MARCH 5, 1821: The second inauguration of James Monroe. Location: The Capitol's House Chamber. The ceremony occurs on the fifth because the fourth falls on a Sunday.

MARCH 4, 1825: The inauguration of the sixth U.S. president, John Quincy Adams, a former Massachusetts state senator and U.S. senator, who previously had been the chief U.S. negotiator of the Treaty of Ghent, which ended the War of 1812; and secretary of state (under Monroe). Location: The Capitol's House Chamber. Like his father, John Adams, John Quincy Adams was never a slaveholder.

DECEMBER 22, 1825: An unattended candle causes a fire in the Congressional Library, then housed in a room in the Capitol's west wing.

1826: The First Presbyterian Church, at the foot of Capitol Hill, starts holding classes for blacks on Sunday evenings. Decades later, a report on schools will state that at this church "many men and women, as well as children, learned their alphabet and to read the Bible. Michael Shiner, one of the most remarkable colored men of the District . . . is of this number." The church building will become the home of Israel Bethel, an African Methodist Episcopal church.

JANUARY 18, 1827: "The dispatch came from Alexandria . . . to the people of Washington early in the morning calling on them to come down speedily to assist in putting the fire out. And orders came from the Navy department the same morning . . . [for] Commander Thomas Tingey to send every mechanic and laborer and engine out of the Yard and every man that was able to travel." The Navy Yard sends some three hundred men to Alexandria on that freezing cold day (13 degrees!). Shiner and the other men march over frozen ground "in a half canter and a dog trot." This horrific fire starts in a cabinetmaker's shop near the intersection of Royal and King Streets and destroys more than fifty homes and businesses.

APRIL 29, 1828: The U.S. Capitol Police are established.

MARCH 4, 1829: The inauguration of the seventh U.S. president, Andrew Jackson, a Tennessee slave-holder regarded by many as a great hero for his victory in the War of 1812's Battle of New Orleans (which took place after the peace treaty was signed—news traveled slowly) and for his Indian fighting over the years. Location: The Capitol's East Portico.

APRIL 13, 1832: Sam Houston, the future "father of Texas," runs into Ohio representative William Stanbery on Pennsylvania Avenue and begins beating him with his hickory cane. Houston's attack is in retaliation for recent insults on the House floor. In self-defense, Stanbery pulls a gun, but it misfires. After hitting Stanbery some more, Houston continues on his way to the theater. He will face no jail time, only a reprimand and a fine.

MARCH 4, 1833: The second inauguration of Andrew Jackson. Location: The Capitol's House Chamber.

MARCH 30, 1833: The U.S. Treasury Building burns down. "You could see the paper flying in the air from the building."

SEPTEMBER 26, 1833: Concerned citizens meet in City Hall about Congress's failure to act on the years-long proposal for the capital to have a monument honoring George Washington. From this meeting is born the Washington National Monument Society. Its mission: to raise money for the project. George Watterston, former chief of the Congressional Library, will serve as secretary of the organization.

President's Levee; or, All Creation Going to the White House, aquatint by Robert Cruikshank from *The Playfair Papers; or, Brother Jonathan, the Smartest Nation in All Creation,* volume 2 (1841), by Hugo Playfair. Andrew Jackson made his first inaugural reception an open house. The crowd was so large—and the alcohol so plentiful—that things got a bit wild and the President's House saw some damage.

*Two weeks have passed since we located ourselves in our new habitation
[on Fifteenth Street NW]. . . . Our house, a delightful one, [is] in the best part
of the city, surrounded by good neighbors, good churches, and good pavement which enable us to visit both neighbors and churches in all weather. . . .
A broad pavement leads one way to Capitol Hill and another to George-Town,
besides cross paved ways in every direction. We could keep up a very social
intercourse now without a carriage. . . . Mrs. Clay, Mrs. Southard, Mrs. Lovel,
Mrs. Cutts . . . Mrs. Rush, Mrs. Wirt, Mrs. Thornton, are our neighbors. . . .*

—Margaret Bayard Smith, November 21, 1828

This famous white Washington chronicler had moved to the capital in 1800 with her husband,
Samuel Harrison Smith, founder of the newspaper that became the *Daily National Intelligencer*.

3

AN AX,
A "SNOW-STORM,"
LUNCH BASKETS,
★ AND ★
BRICKBATS

Brown's Indian Queen Hotel, Washington City (c. 1832), lithograph, published by W. Endicott & Co. This grand hotel was on Pennsylvania Avenue between Sixth and Seventh Streets NW, midway between the President's House and the Capitol. It was a favorite haunt of politicians, and some members of Congress and the Supreme Court lived there while in town.

WHEN SHINER'S WIFE AND DAUGHTERS GAINED

their liberty, Washington was still a long way from being a splendid and beautiful city—but it wasn't an absolute wasteland. Yes, there were still mud holes, but there were also theater and teas, chess parties, and feasts, where the elite talked politics or sometimes just engaged in mindless chitchat over pickled oysters.

Local merchants carried all manner of goods, from china to gilt-framed mirrors. And books—such as *Village Belles*, a novel in two volumes ($1.25 in 1833), and the *Cyclopedia of Practical Medicine and Surgery* (50 cents per volume). For those in need not of a medical journal but of medicine itself, there was W. Gunton, for one, hawking remedies, such as Dr. Church's Vermifuge Lozenges (for worms "in children and grown persons," at 37½ cents per box).

But when it came to mores and morals, the capital left a lot to be desired. People opposed to slavery continued to condemn the city for allowing it, just as they vilified its slaveholders, its slave pens, and its slave dealers—such as Simpson and Neal, whose ads read: "We will at all times pay higher prices in cash for likely young Negroes, of both sexes, either in families or otherwise, than any other purchasers who are now or may hereafter come into this market."

Local newspapers also carried ads about people who escaped slavery—men like Edmond. He was about thirty-two years old in July 1833, when he broke free from John Walden in Virginia. Walden described Edmond thus: "About five feet ten inches high; his complexion is rather a deep brown; his hair long and combed erect; his visage is sharp, and when spoken to has a downcast look and is rather blunt in his manner." For Edmond's return, Walden offered a hundred-dollar reward if he was captured outside Virginia, fifty dollars if in Virginia, and twenty-five if in Walden's county (Fauquier). In any event, Edmond was to be held until Walden could "reduce him to possession."

While abolitionists were pained by such items and by the whole beastly business of slavery in the capital, they couldn't honestly be shocked. After all, the district was carved out of two slave states, and five of the nation's first seven presidents were slaveholders. There were more than a few others who served in the national government who were slaveholders—such as former Vice President John C. Calhoun, of South Carolina.

Washington had its fair share of less heinous wrongs. On June 7, 1833, the day that Shiner made those three trips across the Long Bridge, some miscreant stole a sorrel mare from Richard Wright's stable behind a church on Ninth Street NW. About a month later, Ann Maria Myers's store at Pennsylvania and Third NW was broken into "and the money drawer, containing between 20 and 30 dollars, taken."

Like other cities, the capital had nativists, American-born whites who harbored hatred for European immigrants, particularly Roman Catholics, and particularly the

Irish. But the animosity toward white foreigners ranked below that for blacks, especially free blacks. People like schoolteacher John Francis Cook.

Free blacks were seen as trouble, as bad examples. They were examples of freedom, filling blacks in bondage with dreams of

John Francis Cook (c. 1840), photographer unknown. Cook was born in slavery and had his aunt Alethia Browning Tanner to thank for his freedom. She bought several family members out of slavery with money she made selling vegetables in Lafayette Square. John Cook, a shoemaker by trade, opened his school, Union Seminary, in 1834. He would later help found the First Colored Presbyterian Church, the seed of today's Fifteenth Street Presbyterian Church.

Anna Marie Brodeau Thornton (1804), oil on canvas, by Gilbert Stuart. Thornton was twenty-nine when she sat for this portrait.

liberty by, if nothing else, their mere presence. Too, whites rightly assumed that some free blacks not only encouraged enslaved blacks to take their liberty but also helped them to do it. In the summer of 1835, the anti-black sentiment turned violent. Evil grew wings.

The trouble began on August 8, when a white mob stormed to the city jail intent on lynching eighteen-year-old Arthur Bowen. With his mother, Maria, Arthur was one of several people held in slavery by socialite

Anna Thornton, widow of William Thornton, architect of the first Capitol.

Like Shiner, Arthur Bowen was strong-willed; he refused to be an "obedient slave." He gambled (billiards, horse races) and sometimes got drunk. He had a serious side, however. He wanted a better life—wanted out of slavery—and had been dropping in on meetings of an organization John Francis Cook had started: the Philomathean Talking Society, devoted to philomathy (from the Greek for "love of learning"). Learning about the abolitionist movement was high on the list for the society's members. Handouts included copies of anti-slavery newspapers, such as the *Liberator*.

When Bowen left a meeting on August 4, he idled on the streets with a friend, breaking the ten o'clock curfew imposed on blacks, which was punishable by a ten-dollar fine and possibly a night in jail. It was past midnight when Bowen, tipsy, returned to the Thornton town house on F Street NW, a few blocks from the President's House. Anna Thornton awoke to find the young man standing in the doorway of her bedroom. He had an ax in the crook of his arm.

Rumor was that Bowen "was going to knock his mistress in the head with that ax," remembered Michael Shiner. Rumor was that the city had a Nat Turner! "I'll have my freedom, you hear me?" Arthur shouted after his mother hurried him out of Thornton's house.

The first fruit.—*A circumstance of a shocking character . . . occurred in this city two nights ago, which, viewing it as one of the effects of the fanatical spirit of the day, and one of the immediate fruits of the incendiary [antislavery] publications with which this city and the whole slave-holding portion of the country have been lately inundated, we have concluded it to be our duty to make public. On Tuesday night last, an attempt was made on the life of Mrs. Thornton . . . by a Negro man, her slave, which, from the expressions he used, was evidently induced by reading the inflammatory publications referred above.*

—*Daily National Intelligencer*, August 7, 1835

Bowen came out of hiding a few days later, on August 8, and was hustled into the city jail. There, as Michael Shiner put it, a mob swore to "pull the jail down," aiming to hang Bowen "without judge or juror." Marines from the Navy Yard were soon on the scene, and "they done their duty without faction or favor," remembered Michael Shiner.

Some whites in Washington were soon clamoring for the head of Reuben Crandall, a visiting white physician whose sister, Prudence Crandall, had run a school for black girls in Connecticut. Like his sister, Reuben was an abolitionist, and when, on August 10, anti-slavery material was found in his Georgetown lodgings, he was hauled off to the city jail where Arthur Bowen still languished. Reuben Crandall was charged with circulating material bound to incite a rebellion like Nat Turner's.

Meanwhile, as Arthur Bowen and Reuben Crandall sat in the city jail, fearing for their lives, "there was a rumor flying around about a colored man by the name of Snow," remembered Shiner. He was referring to thirty-six-year-old Beverly Randolph Snow, a Virginian. After Snow's last owner freed him, in 1829, he and his wife, Julia (freed earlier by her owner), headed for Washington. In partnership with another black man, William Walker, Beverly Snow opened a restaurant. Its final location was on the corner of Sixth Street and Pennsylvania Avenue NW, in a building down the street from Brown's Indian Queen Hotel. Snow's place was no run-of-the-mill eatery but one of the capital's "first true restaurants . . . if not the very first," according to journalist Jefferson Morley.

Snow named his place the Epicurean Eating House out of his fondness for Epicurus, an ancient Greek philosopher who believed that avoiding pain and distress should be everyone's goal and that pleasure in moderation—such as the savoring of good food—was most excellent for the soul. Roast pheasant, canvasback duck, and green turtle soup were among the delights served at the Epicurean Eating House. It was not a place Shiner could afford.

And that rumor? That this black restaurateur, whose patrons included prominent politicians, had said nasty things about white women whose menfolk worked at the Yard.

When Snow got wind that a gang was coming for him, he "flew for his life," recalled Shiner. Unable to get Snow in their clutches, the mob attacked the Epicurean Eating House. They "busted up" the place, "root and branch."

That was the start of a three-day rampage called the "Snow-Storm" or the "Snow Riot." Whites attacked and sacked black homes, schools, and businesses. Casualties included John Cook's school on Fourteenth and H Streets NW. The rioters "marched into his schoolhouse, destroyed all the books and furniture and partially destroyed the building," wrote another Washingtonian, Moses B. Goodwin.

"Parents, guardians, and others, are earnestly requested to keep their children, apprentices, &c. within doors after dusk," urged Mayor William Bradley in a proclamation issued on August 12.

★ ★ ★

Many people contend that the news of ax-holding Arthur Bowen sparked the riot, but something Shiner wrote suggests that the truth wasn't that simple. He recalled that the night after Snow's restaurant was busted up, members of the mob, composed mostly of Yard workers, "threatened to come to the Navy Yard after Commodore Hull."

THE LIBERATOR.

VOL. V.]   OUR COUNTRY IS THE WORLD—OUR COUNTRYMEN ARE ALL MANKIND.   [NO. 35.

BOSTON, MASSACHUSETTS.   [SATURDAY, AUGUST 29, 1835.

Destruction by Fire of Pennsylvania Hall on the Night of the 17th May, 1838 (1838), lithograph, by J. C. Wild. Pennsylvania Hall, built by the Pennsylvania Anti-Slavery Society, was torched by a white mob a few days after its dedication. As the ranks of abolitionists grew in the 1830s, so did the number of people willing to thwart their efforts by hook or by crook. The anti-black and anti-abolitionist riots that broke out in cities around the nation in the 1830s were sometimes stirred up by members of the working class, members of the middle class, and members of the elite.

Blacks and white abolitionists were certainly the targets of white Washingtonians' rage, and, in this, Washington resembled the rest of the country—there were dozens of anti-black and anti-abolitionist riots around the nation in the 1830s. However, during the capital's dog days of 1835—days during which Shiner surely feared for his life—deep job dissatisfaction was at the root of the Yard workers' fury. Commandant Hull had pushed them over the edge.

Back on July 29, Hull had issued a two-pronged order stating that (1) during lunchtime, mechanics (skilled workers) and laborers (unskilled workers) could no longer enter workshops and other buildings in the Yard where tools and other supplies were kept, and (2) these workers could

Isaac Hull (1834), oil on canvas, by Samuel L. Waldo, after Gilbert Stuart. In the War of 1812, Hull was captain of the USS *Constitution*. Like Thomas Tingey, this Connecticut native had enslaved people working as his personal servants at the Yard. When he replaced Tingey, he was not at all pleased with the condition of the Yard: pocked with holes and gullies, timber strewn about, docks caving in—it was "in an awful condition," remembered Shiner. Commandant Hull got the Yard shipshape; he had sheds built, fences put up, and repairs made.

aware that, two days before Hull issued his order, a blacksmith's striker in the Yard's anchor shop was caught slipping a copper spike into his lunch basket. When the man's house was searched, more government property was found.

The mechanics and the laborers "got insulted" by Hull's order, recalled Shiner. These men were already disgusted with the low wages and the twelve-hour workdays. Most of them were day laborers, so if on a particular day, because of gale-force winds or a blizzard, there was no work, then there was no pay for most of them, either. And now Hull was basically calling them a pack of thieves. In response, 175 white carpenters, blacksmiths, and other skilled and unskilled workers—75 percent of the Yard's workforce—went on strike. But not the free black workers. Not at first.

By Shiner's count, there were fifteen or twenty black caulkers working on the *Columbia*, a fifty-gun frigate. Like their foreman, Israel Jones, these men had been brought in from Baltimore. It nettled white Yard workers that black men had those good jobs. And those white men weren't about to let black men continue earning money

no longer bring their lunches "in baskets, bags, or otherwise" into the Yard without permission. Hull's aim was to stop the stealing that was going on. This was something Shiner was well aware of—just as he was while they were on strike. They forced the black caulkers to, as Shiner put it, "knock off, too."

Earlier in the year, shipyard workers in other cities had dropped their tools, but the Washington Navy Yard strike was the first against the federal government. As at other shipyards, the number-one demand at the Washington Navy Yard was a ten-hour workday.

The Washington Navy Yard workers never stormed Commandant Hull, which didn't surprise Shiner. He thought it was just talk to antagonize Hull. Not working agonized the striking workers—and their families. There was no union and so no rainy-day fund for workers to draw on while on strike, and most had no savings of their own.

On August 15, 1835, the strike was over. The workers hadn't won that ten-hour day, but they had regained the right to bring their lunch baskets into the Yard. And they were soon free of Hull. A few weeks after the strike ended, he was granted a leave of absence, which became permanent.

★ ★ ★

The trial of Arthur Bowen, charged with attempted murder, began on Thursday,

Francis Scott Key (1816 or after), oil on canvas, attributed to Joseph Wood. Key served as the U.S. attorney for the District of Columbia from 1833 to 1841. He lived in Georgetown.

December 10, 1835. The attorney prosecuting him—and seeking the death penalty—was Francis Scott Key, who twenty years earlier had written the poem that became a very popular song and would one day be the U.S. national anthem.

On January 23, 1836, Key got the verdict and the sentence he sought. For standing in a white woman's bedroom door with an ax—but not harming a hair on her head—Arthur Bowen was condemned to die. His date of execution was set for February 26. He was to be hanged.

Though a slaveholder, Anna Thornton wasn't without some conscience. She had long believed that Bowen had simply been drunk and stupid, not out for blood, and she petitioned President Andrew Jackson to pardon him. Her petition was successful. After Bowen's release, Thornton sold the young man to someone who then sold him to a man in the transportation business (steamboats and stagecoaches). Whether Arthur Bowen and his mother ever saw each other again is a mystery.

And Reuben Crandall? In April 1836, he was acquitted and set free. He promptly left the capital.

As for Beverly Snow, he was long gone, having sworn in writing that he had never said nasty things about white women. Trooper that he was, he remained a restaurateur. In Toronto, Canada.

★ ★ ★

And Shiner?

A few weeks after the so-called Snow Riot, Shiner, who had not been out of the Yard for more than three weeks, went on a one-man riot of his own, after promising a marine, from whom he borrowed a dollar, that he would not get drunk.

"I got as tight as I could get pretty near," Shiner confessed in his book. He "got so wild" that he was jumped on Capitol Hill.

Late-nineteenth-century paintbrushes. Their handles are about two feet long. The brushes Shiner used may have looked something like these.

The same thing happened as he careened down Navy Yard Hill and beyond—"They pelted me with stones and brickbats!" At the end of the day, Shiner was in the "lock up house," and the next day, before a judge.

Yet again, Shiner escaped punishment. Seeing not a scratch on the people there to testify against this man, the judge released him. Back to the Yard went Michael Shiner, by now assigned to the paint shop.

That was Shiner's last account of being drunk and disorderly, behavior very possibly rooted in pent-up rage over being enslaved. Though he had more day-to-day liberty than other people in captivity elsewhere in the South and even right there in the capital, Shiner was never his own man. He had to live with that painful reality every day of his life. But then one day he stopped drinking, never specifying his motivation. He only declared that on Sunday, December 4, 1836, he made a sea change: "I never have had a drop of liquor in my mouth since that time of no kind." It may well have been Shiner's way of toasting liberty.

Earlier that year, Michael Shiner was resourceful enough to do as other enslaved people in the capital and elsewhere had done: he sued for his freedom. His advocate was a man of consequence: future District Attorney for the District of Columbia, James Hoban Jr., a son of the first architect of the President's House.

On March 26, 1836, in the Circuit Court of the District of Columbia for Washington County, Hoban filed a petition for freedom, stating that Shiner was "unjustly, and illegally held in bondage"

by the executors of Thomas Howard Sr.'s estate. Shiner may well have gotten wind of the plot to have the manumission promised in Howard's will set aside.

In Shiner's case, the paper trail goes cold, suggesting that the matter was settled out of court.

Shiner was definitely nobody's slave by the summer of 1840, when the federal census was taken. He, now in his mid-thirties, is found under "Free Colored Persons."

The Saturday, March 26, 1836, summons for Ann Nancy Howard and William E. Howard to appear in court on Monday, March 28, "to answer to the Petition of Freedom of Michael Shiner, filed in said Circut against them." She was the chief clerk's widow, and he was one of their sons. They were co-executors of Thomas Howard's estate—that is, the people responsible for carrying out the wishes of the deceased.

District of Columbia, TO WIT:

THE UNITED STATES OF AMERICA,

To the Marshal of the District of Columbia, GREETING:

You are hereby commanded to summon *Ann Howard &*
William E. Howard, Executors of
Thomas Howard
if *they* shall be found in the County of Washington,
that (all excuses set aside) *they* be and appear before
the Circuit Court of the District of Columbia, to be held
for the County of Washington, in the City of Washington, on *fourth Mon-*
day of *March next* next, to testify on the part of *to answer*
the Petition for freedom of Michael Shiner, filed
in said Court against them.

Hereof, fail not at your peril; and have you then and there this **Precept.**

Witness, *W Cranch* —Esquire, Chief Judge of the said Court.

Issued the *25th* day of *March* 1836.

CAPITAL DAYS
★TIMELINE★

The location for all presidential inaugurations was the Capitol's East Portico, except in the case of John Tyler.

JANUARY 30, 1835: As President Andrew Jackson leaves a funeral in the Capitol, a white out-of-work housepainter named Richard Lawrence tries to shoot him, but his derringers misfire. Lawrence, who believes himself to be British royalty, is the first person tried for attempting to assassinate a U.S. president. He is found innocent by reason of insanity and will die in 1861 in the Government Hospital for the Insane (renamed St. Elizabeth's in 1916).

AUGUST 25, 1835: Service starts on the Washington branch of the Baltimore & Ohio Railroad. "A whole passel of people went and the councilmen and aldermen went free passage to Baltimore and back. Among those passengers was Sailing Master Marmaduke Dove." The B&O depot in the capital is at Pennsylvania Avenue and Second Street NW.

MAY 25, 1836: "Am I gagged or am I not?" shouts former president John Quincy Adams, now a Massachusetts representative. Adams is responding to being shouted down in the House by proslavery representatives pushing for a resolution to ignore petitions calling for the abolition of slavery in the District of Columbia, petitions that are mounting daily. The next day, the House passes this pledge: "Resolved, that all petitions, memorials, resolutions, propositions, or papers, relating in any way or to any extent whatever to the subject of slavery, or the abolition of slavery, shall, without being either printed or referred, be laid upon the table, and that no further action whatever shall be had thereon." This resolution is the first of several that become known as gag rules.

But I take higher ground. I hold that in the present state of civilization, where two races of different origin, and distinguished by color, and other physical differences, as well as intellectual, are brought together, the relation now existing in the slaveholding States between the two, is, instead of an evil, a good—a positive good. . . . And I here fearlessly assert that the existing relation between the two races in the South, against which these blind fanatics [abolitionists] are waging war, forms the most solid and durable foundation on which to rear free and stable political institutions.

—South Carolina Senator John C. Calhoun,
February 6, 1837

In his speech on the Senate floor, Calhoun called for the Senate to adopt a gag rule as the House had done.

JULY 4, 1836: Congress approves the construction of a new Treasury Building—to be fireproof.

MARCH 4, 1837: The inauguration of the eighth U.S. president, Martin Van Buren, a former vice president (in Jackson's second term). Van Buren grew up on a farm in Kinderhook, New York, that was worked in part by slave labor, and he held at least one person in slavery. However, he was opposed to slavery for most of his life.

1837–38: Congress receives upwards of 130,000 petitions for the abolition of slavery and of the slave trade in the capital, and about 180,000 petitions protesting the proposed annexation of the Republic of Texas (land that once belonged to Mexico), because Texas is dead set on entering the Union as a slave state.

MARCH 31, 1840: President Van Buren mandates a ten-hour workday for laborers and mechanics employed on public works. Reflecting on the men at work on the Treasury Building (completed in 1842) "in the hot broiling sun from sun to sun," Shiner declared that the president's name "ought to be recorded in every workingman's heart."

MARCH 4, 1841: The inauguration of the ninth U.S president, William Henry Harrison. "Slush and snow on the ground." Harrison, the son of a signer of the Declaration of Independence, a Virginia landowner with many slaves, was himself at one point a slave-holder, converting slaves into "indentured servants" when on free soil, as when serving as governor of Indiana Territory. Harrison wasn't wearing a coat or a hat when he delivered his Inaugural Address—the longest yet, lasting close to two hours.

APRIL 4, 1841: President Harrison dies of pneumonia after a month in office.

APRIL 6, 1841: Vice President John Tyler, a Virginia slaveholder, is sworn in as president. Location: Brown's Indian Queen Hotel, where he has been living.

Scene in the Slave Pen at Washington, from Solomon Northup's memoir, *Twelve Years a Slave* (1853). "Again and again I asserted I was no man's slave," wrote Northup in the passage in his book on his confinement and abuse in William H. Williams's jail.

APRIL 8, 1841: Thirty-three-year-old Solomon Northup, a black man born free in New York State, is kidnapped in the capital and held in William H. Williams's jail, known as the Yellow House, in the vicinity of what is now the National Mall. Northup, a husband and the father of three, is soon shipped to Louisiana. He will endure twelve years in bondage there. Two white men had lured Northup to the capital with the promise of work as a musician with a traveling circus.

It is sometimes called the City of Magnificent Distances, but it might with greater propriety be termed the City of Magnificent Intentions. . . . Spacious avenues that begin in nothing, and lead nowhere; streets, mile-long, that only want houses, roads, and inhabitants; public buildings that need but a public to be complete; and ornaments of great thoroughfares, which only lack great thoroughfares to ornament—are its leading features. . . . It has no trade or commerce of its own: having little or no population beyond the President and his establishment; the members of the legislature who reside there during the session; the Government clerks and officers employed in the various departments; the keepers of the hotels and boarding-houses; and the tradesmen who supply their tables. It is very unhealthy. Few people would live in Washington, I take it, who were not obliged to reside there. . . . There is a very pleasant and commodious library in the Capitol.

—Charles Dickens

The celebrated English writer toured America in 1842.

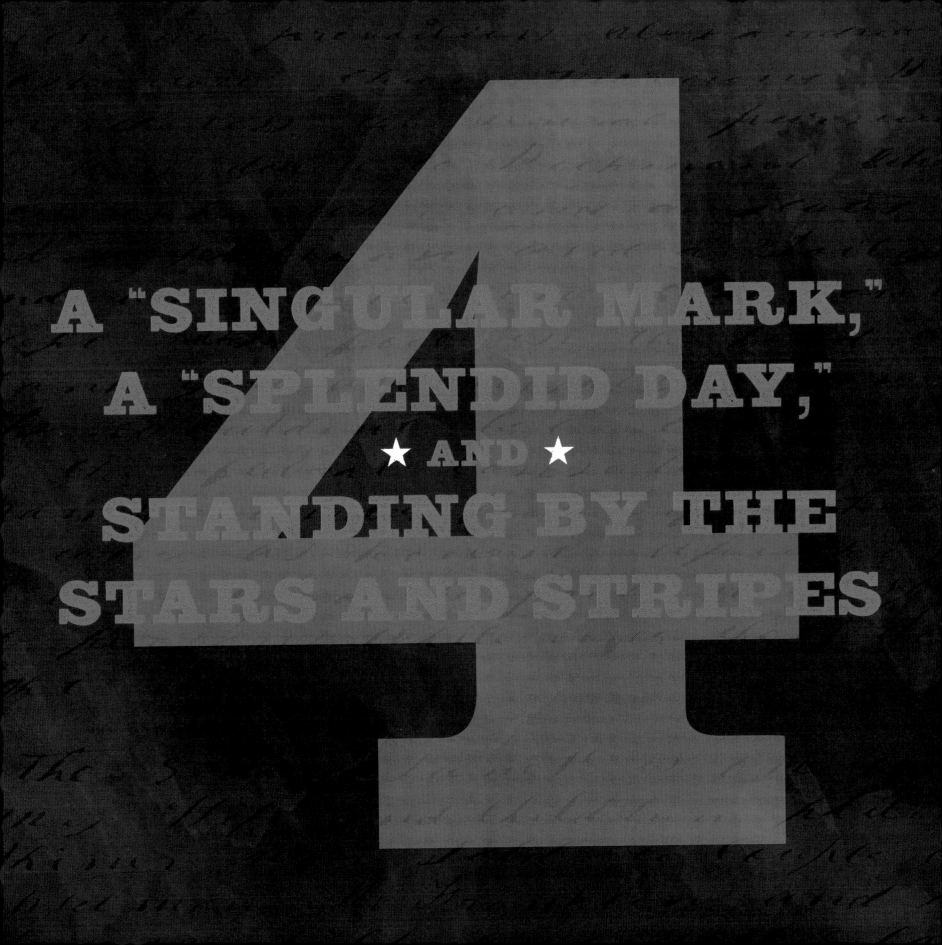

A "SINGULAR MARK," A "SPLENDID DAY," ★ AND ★ STANDING BY THE STARS AND STRIPES

Capitol and Part of Washington City (1839), ink and ink wash, over graphite underdrawing, by Augustus Köllner. The Capitol had been completed more than ten years earlier, in 1826.

FLY! NO, THAT'S NOT WHAT MICHAEL SHINER did when he became a free man. Instead of moving to Pennsylvania or another state where slavery had been abolished, he remained in the capital, where laws called black codes (which also existed in the North), though enforced willy-nilly, put limits on the liberty of free blacks. Black codes became even more repressive after the "Snow Riot," even though whites had been the violent ones.

By law, Shiner couldn't have a big get-together in his home without a permit.

Couldn't own a tavern or any kind of eatery.

Couldn't get a license to be in any business other than driving "carts, drays, hackney carriages or wagons, and huckstering."

Couldn't be "idle without any visible means" of support. For that he could be fined up to thirty dollars or kicked out of the capital.

Having a job wasn't a problem for Shiner. He kept working in the Navy Yard paint shop: grinding colors, mixing paint, toting paint, painting ships and structures. His pay was about two dollars a day, now all his, money with which to support himself and his family—a family that after 1833 fades from *Michael Shiner His Book*. In fact, Shiner says less and less about his life and more about the people around him.

Saturday, February 22, 1840: Boatswain David Eaton, before whose home Shiner once planted an apple tree, dies at age sixty-one—"as great a seaman as ever stepped his foot on a ship's deck."

Tuesday, September 7, 1841: Marine Rifle Corps captain and master armorer Jacob Bright dies when a thirty-two-pound shell explodes in the Yard.

Monday, June 27, 1842: Another explosion at the Yard kills two more men.

Reflecting on these three deaths in ten months, Shiner mused: "We are all neglectful of the things that are most needful for our souls welfare. For when we part from each other for our daily occupation we don't know whether we will ever return in life again."

An even greater explosion rocked the capital twenty months later, on Wednesday, February 28, 1844. The sun was warm on that winter day. All was swell for a pleasure cruise celebrating the launch of the USS *Princeton*, the world's first steam warship with a screw propeller (as opposed to a paddlewheel, which had replaced sails as the main means of propulsion).

President John Tyler was among the hundreds of VIPs aboard the *Princeton*, with wine and champagne and merriment flowing. But during a display of armaments, the biggest cannon, the 27,000-pound "Peacemaker," exploded.

The dead included Secretary of State Abel Upshur and Secretary of the Navy Thomas Gilmer. President Tyler was among the many who escaped injury.

Awful Explosion of the "Peace-maker" on Board the U.S. Steam Frigate, Princeton, *on Tuesday, 28th Feby. 1844* (1844), hand-colored lithograph, published by N. Currier, New York. More than a half-dozen people died and about twenty were wounded.

Upon turning my eyes towards [the Peace-maker] I was astonished to find that every man between me and the gun was lying prostrate on the deck—and about 30 or 40 men lying in heaps . . . either killed, wounded, or knocked down and stunned by the concussion as the smoke gradually cleared away. . . . My eye next caught three gentlemen struck down almost by my side by a fragment of the gun . . . from whom as well as the others the blood was running in crimson streams. . . . I discovered that the middle one of the three was [Secretary of the Navy Thomas Gilmer].

—New Jersey Representative George Sykes, March 1844

Earlier on the day of the catastrophe, Shiner had been filled with foreboding when he saw something odd in the sky. "Come here and look at this singular mark across the elements," he said to an acquaintance.

"I never saw anything like that before," the man responded.

"The Lord have mercy on us," said Shiner. "Something's surely going to happen."

Something terrible almost happened to *him* two years later, on the morning of February 12, 1846. There was yet another explosion at the Yard, this one in its laboratory, where shells and other explosive devices were made. Remembered Shiner: "I hadn't left there more than fifteen minutes . . . and I had been there twice that morning and used to very often go to the furnace to warm myself." The explosion brought instant death to a young man Shiner called "Dalas" and the *Daily National Intelligencer* called Daily, a native of Philadelphia, "whose skull and head were shattered in a dreadful manner."

And yet, Shiner's book wasn't a litany of disasters. June 7, 1848, was a capital day for him. He was among the Yard workers who volunteered their brains and brawn for the rescue of a nearly 25,000-pound block of Maryland marble that had fallen from a wagon and through the Fourteenth Street bridge. It was to be the base for a monument to America's first president.

After the Yard workers got the Washington Monument's cornerstone onto another vehicle, they "walked off with it handsomely," remembered Michael Shiner. As the *Daily National Intelligencer* pointed out, what he and his coworkers did was no cheap show of patriotism. They "sacrificed

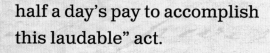

half a day's pay to accomplish this laudable" act.

A few weeks later, on the Fourth of July 1848, Shiner was in a crowd of twenty thousand for the dedication of that cornerstone. "There was a great procession that day!" he recalled: "different volunteer companies and the United States dragoons from Carlisle Barracks, Pennsylvania, three or four companies of them under the command of lieutenant-colonel Charles May, United States Army, and one battery of flying artillery, and several volunteer companies from Alexandria—" He summed it up as a "splendid day," capped by a "good display of fireworks" that night.

★ ★ ★

Fires continued to plague the city: "The library of the United States Capitol was burnt on the 24th of December 1851 (a Wednesday) and all the

Present Staff of the Monument at Washington (1853), hand-colored wood engraving that originally appeared in the January 8, 1853, issue of *Illustrated News*. The 555-foot-tall obelisk won't be completed until 1884.

engineers and the mechanics and laborers out of the Navy Yard was ordered to the Capitol . . . to assist putting the fire out." It was about eight o'clock in the morning when the captain of the Capitol Police smelled fire, reported the *National Era*. "The Library of Congress," lamented the newspaper, "with its rich collection of valuable books, public documents, precious manuscripts, paintings, busts, medals, and other works of art, is in ashes." The library lost two-thirds of its collection (including about 35,000 books). It would not reopen until August 1853.

By then, Shiner had seen another cornerstone dedicated, this one on the Fourth of July 1851 for the expansion of the Capitol. The nation's growth to thirty-one states—sixteen free, fifteen slave—meant more U.S. senators and representatives. They needed a larger place to convene.

By the time work on the Capitol was under way, Shiner had suffered a personal loss and had a new beginning: his wife Phillis had died, and he had remarried, in 1849. The woman was Jane Jackson, herself a widow.

The 1850 federal census tells us that as of late July of that year, the Shiners lived in Ward Six. Michael, in his mid-forties, was head of a household that included his wife Jane, nineteen; Sarah E., twelve; Isaac M., five; and baby boy Braxton, six months old. Given that Jane was only nineteen, young Sarah and Isaac were most likely children Phillis had had after her first three daughters, Ann, Harriet, and Mary Ann, who were all grown women by 1850.

By then, the Washington Navy Yard, like other parts of the capital, was poised for upgrades. Shiner chronicled pile drivings, along with first stones and bricks laid, for a bunch of new buildings—a copper rolling mill, a sawmill, a blacksmith's shop, an ordnance building. The manufacturing of ordnance, mostly cannons and shells, was now the Yard's stock-in-trade (hence, all those explosions).

John Dahlgren was the man who put the Yard on the map as an ordnance manufacturer. His inventions and innovations, such as the bottle-shaped smoothbore cannon, earned him the nickname "father of U.S. naval ordnance."

When he was assigned to the Yard in 1847, Dahlgren probably never imagined that his weapons would one day be aimed at fellow Americans. But that's what happened when tensions between pro-slavery and anti-slavery forces reached, as Shiner would say, the "explosion part."

★ ★ ★

For a slew of the roughly 400,000 slaveholders in fifteen of the thirty-three states, the fuse was lit when Abraham Lincoln won the presidency in November 1860. The sixteenth president, never a slaveholder, truly detested slavery and spoke boldly about curbing its expansion. In turn, people who approved of slavery detested Lincoln: they feared he would crusade to end it everywhere in the nation. Slaveholders in South Carolina feared it so much that they rallied their state to secede from the United States.

It did, on December 20, 1860. The South Carolina legislature then issued an address urging other states to do the same: "We ask you to join us in forming a Confederacy of Slaveholding States." Several states heeded that call—and the nation exploded into a civil war.

Friday, April 12, 1861: Secessionists attack Fort Sumter, in South Carolina's Charleston Harbor.

Sunday, April 14, 1861: The Stars and Stripes atop Fort Sumter is struck. The flag that takes its place, the Stars and Bars, hails the Confederate States of America, the seven slaveholding states that have seceded: South Carolina, Mississippi, Florida, Alabama, Georgia, Louisiana, and Texas. By mid-June, four more slave states will have joined the Confederacy: Virginia, Arkansas, North Carolina, and Tennessee.

★ ★ ★

With the onset of war, the capital became a very hurry-scurry, high-strung, shove-off-let-fall-give-way! place to be.

Saturday, April 20, 1861: Lincoln orders watercraft on the Potomac to make haste to the Yard—"and they was bringing the boats to the Yard all night Saturday night," remembered Michael Shiner.

Monday, April 22, 1861: "They commenced hauling flour from the different warehouses in Washington, D.C., and Georgetown to the Capitol of the United States." The Capitol, still under construction, serves as a bakery, barracks, and hospital for Union troops.

During these dangerous days, some Washingtonians snatched their children from school and their money from banks, then fled. But not Michael Shiner. He who

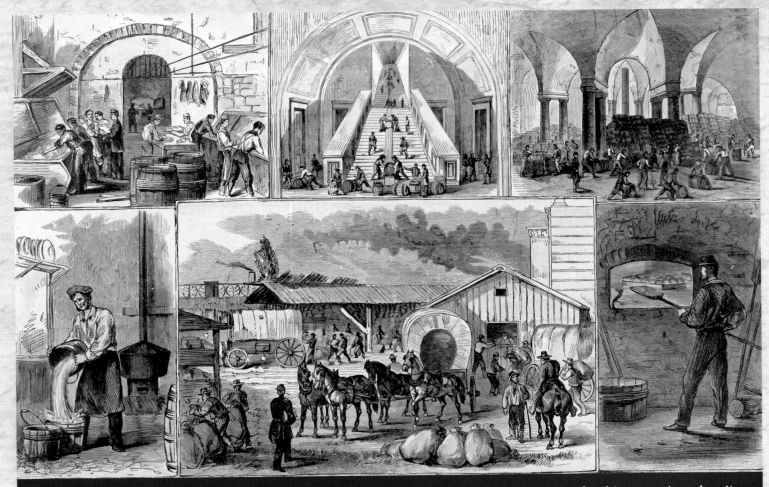

The Great Bakery for the United States Army at the Capitol, Washington, D.C., was the caption for this engraving when it originally appeared in black and white in the September 20, 1862, issue of *Frank Leslie's Illustrated Newspaper*.

had nobody to hold him back this time. He who could easily lose his liberty, if not his life, were the Confederates to invade the capital. He who in the eyes of most Union senators, generals, and other high-ups was a nonentity, a forgettable face in a crowd. He who was deemed unworthy of citizenship, along with other free blacks.

Yet Michael Shiner did not see himself as people of power did. He regarded himself as an American, from stem to stern. Despite its centuries of contempt for people of African descent, America was, nevertheless, a beloved country for Shiner.

And Saturday, June 1, 1861, was a banner day for him. That's when Justice William

The Washington Navy-Yard, with Shad Fishers in the Foreground (1861), hand color-tinted engraving, from the April 20, 1861, issue of *Harper's Weekly*. This view is from the southern side of the Eastern Branch. The buildings are (left to right): ship house, joiners shop, timber shed, and mould loft and forge shop (no wonder so much smoke billows from it); at the far right is the boat house.

Clark arrived at the Yard to secure from about four hundred civilian workers an oath "to stand by the Stars and Stripes and defend for the Union," as Shiner put it. "And I believe at that time, that I, Michael Shiner, was the first colored man that took the oath in Washington, D.C." Now in his mid-fifties, he intended to keep that oath until he died.

★ ★ ★

Just as war had come to Shiner's world in 1814, when he was a boy, so it came when he was a grown man.

On Monday, July 11, 1864, three years into the war, about twenty thousand Confederate soldiers under the command of General Jubal Early launched an attack on the capital. The key was Fort Stevens, which guarded Washington from the north, a city that at the start of the war had about twenty-three thousand troops in it but only nine thousand in the summer of 1864. Thousands had been deployed to campaigns farther south.

With the capital so vulnerable, all able-bodied men were called upon to defend it.

That included civilian workers at the Yard. Its commandant, John Montgomery, was ordered to send every man "fit for service" to nearby Fort Lincoln, in case Confederates attacked from the east.

Unidentified African American Soldier in Union Uniform (1863–65), hand-colored *carte de visite*-plate tintype, by unknown photographer. During the Civil War, roughly 180,000 black men served in the Union Army, and about 19,000 in the Union Navy.

While Shiner was presumably at Fort Lincoln on the night of July 11, Abraham Lincoln was at Fort Stevens, riding "up and down the lines all night long where the federal troops were fighting"—and the next day in danger. As the president stood on the parapet, Confederate sharpshooters took aim. They failed, however, to even graze him. Confederates also failed to take Fort Stevens. They withdrew that night, not up to tangling with the Union troops dispatched from Virginia to the capital. And that's where Michael Shiner continued to live for many more days.

Michael Shiner was present on Saturday, March 4, 1865, for Lincoln's second inauguration. Before the president stepped out onto the Capitol's East Portico, Shiner was in the waiting crowd, buffeted by wind and rain. Then, "as soon as Mr. Lincoln came out, the wind ceased blowing and the rain ceased raining and the sun came out." Shiner even saw a star over the Capitol. It "shined just as bright as it could be."

Another day that Shiner lived to see was Sunday, April 9, 1865, when, in the Virginia village of Appomattox Court House, the Confederacy's number-one

general, Robert E. Lee, surrendered to the commander of the Union armies, Ulysses S. Grant. But the Union's jubilation over its victory was soon cut short because "the Hon. Abraham Lincoln was assassinated: on the 14th of April (on Good Friday night) at Ford's Theatre in Washington. And he died on the 15th of April 1865 (a Saturday)."

Shiner noted that before Lincoln went to the theater on April 14, he and "his lady"

visited the Yard. It is doubtful that Shiner exchanged words with the president (or Mrs. Lincoln). If he had, he surely would have recorded that in his book.

Shiner also lived to see Wednesday, April 26, 1865, the day Lincoln's assassin, Confederate sympathizer John Wilkes Booth, was tracked down and killed near Port Royal, Virginia. When Booth's corpse was brought to the capital, it was held aboard the USS *Montauk*, an ironclad anchored at the Yard. Some of Booth's alleged and actual accomplices would be detained on this same ship.

One of the people who fell under suspicion was James W. Pumphrey, a grandson of the man who brought Shiner's first wife, Phillis, to Washington as a child and the son of Levi Pumphrey, who manumitted Shiner's family in 1833. James W. Pumphrey was arrested after authorities discovered that it was from his livery that Booth had rented his getaway horse. The stable was on C Street NW, behind the National Hotel, where Booth often stayed when in the capital. In the end, Pumphrey was cleared of any involvement in Booth's plot.

★ ★ ★

Michael Shiner retired from the Washington Navy Yard in 1869, when he was in his sixties. For the next few years it appears he had a construction business. Clients included the city of Washington, which in the fall of 1871 hired him to gravel the street and lay sidewalks on Eleventh Street between Pennsylvania and Maryland Avenues.

Shiner also was involved in local politics after blacks gained citizenship through the Fourteenth Amendment (1868), and black men the national vote through the Fifteenth (1870). What's more, the once harum-scarum Michael Shiner became a law-and-order man. For a time, he was a marshal's aide in Ward Six, where he lived. Later, he was a watchman. His beat was the Eastern Market. There, too, he sold produce grown on land he had purchased in the late 1860s.

Shiner was still walking that beat in the late 1870s, on the lookout for pickpockets and scamps cutting up their shines, when another epidemic struck the nation: smallpox, with its fever and chills, its pustules like chicken pox, its power to kill.

Michael Shiner had survived the War of 1812, hard winters, "the Year Without Summer," a drinking problem, a firecracker crew, soldiers harassing him, a near drowning, a cholera outbreak, the near loss of his family, the "Snow Riot," stones and brickbats, explosions at the Yard, the Civil War. And slavery. But he couldn't beat smallpox. He succumbed to the disease in his home, at 338 Ninth Street SE, on January 16, 1880 (a Friday). According to his death certificate, he was seventy-five.

The next day, page eight of the *Evening Star* ran a short piece on smallpox casualties. It remarked on Shiner's passing. Two days later, page one had more to say. Calling him "a character in his day," the *Evening Star* declared that Michael Shiner "probably had the most retentive memory of anyone in the city, being able to give the name and date of every event which came under his observation, even in his boyhood. He had a distinct recollection of the entry of the British into this city, and often related reminiscences of the invasion."

Among the relics that Shiner left behind was a hickory staff from the USS *Minnesota*, a frigate built at the Yard in the 1850s. Attached to this stick was a bayonet from the War of 1812.

More precious was his book.

In the early 1900s, W. H. Crowly, a U.S. Army captain, had a look at *Michael Shiner His Book*. He scribbled this on a back page: "This book is a very valuable book and it is very interesting. It is worthy of perusal and the author Michael Shiner was a patriot. May he rest in peace."

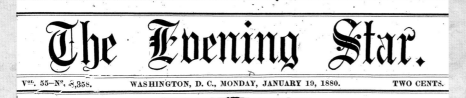

The Evening Star.

Vol. 55—Nº. 8,358.   WASHINGTON, D. C., MONDAY, JANUARY 19, 1880.   TWO CENTS.

THE DEATH OF UNCLE MIKE SHINER.—We briefly stated in Saturday's STAR that Michael Shiner, a well-known colored man, died on Friday night of smallpox. Uncle Mike was a character in his day, and for over half a century was employed in the navy yard as a laborer, working in the paint shop, grinding colors, and he probably had the most retentive memory of any one in the city, being able to give the name and date of every event which came under his observation, even in his boyhood. He had a distinct recollection of the entry of the British into this city, and often related reminiscences of the invasion. He was born here about the year 1800, and until after the emancipation of the colored race occupied his place at the paint mill in the navy yard. Afterwards he became a contractor, and did some work for the corporation and under the board of public works, and took an active part in the local politics of East Washington in suffrage times. For some years past he had been a watchman in the Eastern market.

The *Evening Star*, January 19, 1880. Like many whites at the time, the editors didn't recognize that referring to a black man as "Uncle" or a black woman as "Auntie" was offensive. Perhaps because Shiner lived most of his life in the capital, the newspaper assumed he had been born there. Shiner was buried in Union Beneficial Association Cemetery on C Street between Sixteenth and Seventeenth Streets SE and known as Beckett's Cemetery, a place that is no more.

The Library of Congress, Washington (c. 1905). When the library acquired Shiner's book in 1906, it had been in this building for nine years. The library opened to the public on November 1, 1897. Located on First Street SE, between Independence Avenue and East Capitol Street, this building is now one of several in the Library of Congress complex. In 1980, it was named the Thomas Jefferson Building.

For more than a century *Michael Shiner His Book* has rested among the treasures of an institution that began as a library just for Congress but evolved into America's unofficial national library and the largest library in the world—with more than 150 million items, more than 30 million of them books. Because this library—the Library of Congress—has safeguarded Shiner's book for all these years, one ordinary man has not been lost to history—nor his memories, which add to our knowledge of America's early capital days.

Bird's Eye View—Washington (1869), engraving, by Theodore Davis, from the March 13, 1869, issue of *Harper's Weekly*. It was colored at a later date. This view of the capital reflects the city at the time of the last entry made in Michael Shiner's book.

CAPITAL DAYS
★TIMELINE★

The location for all presidential inaugurations was the Capitol's East Portico, except as noted.

DECEMBER 3, 1844: Largely because of the efforts of John Quincy Adams, the House repeals the gag rule on slavery, imposed in the 1830s. The House can no longer table petitions for the abolition of slavery.

MARCH 4, 1845: The inauguration of the eleventh U.S. president, James K. Polk, a Tennessee slaveholder.

MARCH 5, 1845: "The National Theater burnt down." Fire breaks out during showtime at the ten-year-old theater, three blocks from the President's House.

MAY 13, 1846: Congress says yes to President Polk's request for a declaration of war against Mexico. The cause: a territorial dispute with Mexico over the Texas borderline. When the war ends in 1848, including the annexation of Texas in 1845, Mexico will be reduced to about half its size and the United States will be enlarged by what is now much of its Southwest.

JULY 10, 1846: President Polk signs into law a bill returning to Virginia all parts of the District of Columbia that had originally been ceded by Virginia (some 31 square miles) when the District was created.

AUGUST 10, 1846: President Polk signs into law a bill creating an institution that will be nicknamed the "Nation's Attic"—the Smithsonian. The seed money is from the estate of British scientist James Smithson. The cornerstone of the Smithsonian's first building—"the Castle"—will be laid in spring 1847.

The E.C.Perry Photograph Co.
739 S.BROAD ST. PHILADELPHIA, PA.
473 PENNᵃ AVE. PERMANENT PHOTOGRAPHS WASHINGTON, D.C.

Paul Jennings (c. 1850). He was born in 1799 on James Madison's Virginia plantation, Montpelier. For much of his life, Jennings served as Madison's valet.

SEPTEMBER 28, 1846: Hard up, former First Lady Dolley Madison sells Paul Jennings to an insurance agent for $200. Jennings appeals to Massachusetts Senator Daniel Webster for help. Webster soon buys Jennings for $120, with plans to free him. Jennings is to work off the $120 at a rate of $8 per month.

MAY 8, 1847: "There were a great illuminations and fireworks . . . in the City of Washington celebrating the great battles that were fought in Mexico by Major General Winfield Scott and Major General Zachary Taylor and their officers and men and the man that constructed the fireworks was named Mr. Benjamin Franklin Costern and smarter little fellow as any you could scare up in the United States. And it was a splendid affair."

APRIL 15, 1848: Under cover of night, seventy-seven blacks in the capital and environs, most enslaved, board the *Pearl* at the Seventh Street Wharf, near the Yard. The schooner is to take them on a two-hundred-mile journey to New Jersey, a free state, but the authorities soon capture the *Pearl*. The passengers, along with the ship's white captain and crew, are jailed. The whites will face prison time, and most of the blacks will be sold into slavery in the Deep South.

One of the plan's masterminds was President Madison's former servant Paul Jennings. Another was Daniel Bell, a striker at the Yard, who had bought his freedom the year before (for about $1,600). Bell's wife and children, still in slavery—and about to be sold, he feared—were among the *Pearl*'s passengers. Shiner didn't mention the *Pearl* incident in his book, but he may well have known far more about it than historians know today.

JULY 4, 1848: The cornerstone is laid for the Washington Monument.

MARCH 5, 1849: The inauguration of the twelfth U.S. president, Zachary Taylor, a hero of the Mexican-American War and a Kentucky slaveholder. For the second time, because March 4 falls on a Sunday, the ceremony is held the following day.

JULY 9, 1850: President Taylor dies after sixteen months in office.

JULY 10, 1850: Vice President Millard Fillmore, born in Cayuga County, New York, is sworn in as the thirteenth U.S. president. Location: The Capitol's House Chamber. Fillmore was neither a slaveholder nor an abolitionist.

SEPTEMBER 9–20, 1850: Congress passes the Compromise of 1850, a series of laws designed to keep peace between anti-slavery and pro-slavery forces. These laws include a more muscular Fugitive Slave Act and the abolition of the slave trade—though not of slavery itself—in the District of Columbia.

Be it enacted by the Senate and House of Representatives of the United States of America in Congress assembled, that from and after the first day of January, eighteen hundred and fifty-one, it shall not be lawful to bring into the District of Columbia any slave whatever, for the purpose of being sold, or for the purpose of being placed in depot, to be subsequently transferred to any other State or place to be sold as merchandize. And if any slave shall be brought into the said District by its owner, or by the authority or consent of its owner, contrary to the provisions of this act, such slave shall thereupon become liberated and free.

—Section 1 of the Act to Suppress the Slave Trade
in the District of Columbia

The act was approved by Congress on September 20, 1850, and signed into law by President Millard Fillmore that same day.

MARCH 4, 1853: The inauguration of the fourteenth U.S. president, Franklin Pierce. This New Hampshire native was never a slaveholder.

APRIL 14, 1853: The *Daily National Intelligencer* carries an ad placed by Michael Shiner: "Ran away from Subscriber, on the 10th instant, a mulatto boy named Samuel N. Jackson, about 15 years old, an indented apprentice. Masters of vessels, boats, fishing shores, &c. are hereby forewarned not to harbor, trust, or employ the said boy in any capacity whatever, as the law will be strictly enforced." The fact that Shiner had at least one apprentice suggests that he had some kind of business on the side long before he retired from the Yard. An indentured apprentice was legally bound to work for a set number of years for a master tradesman. For boys, it was typically from age twelve to twenty-one. The apprentice was to be taught a trade and provided with necessities such as food, shelter, and clothing; the employer got free labor. As some employers were brutal, usually only destitute orphans or children from destitute families entered into indentured apprenticeships.

MAY 26, 1854: Congress passes the Kansas-Nebraska Act, and "one hundred guns was fired as a salute. Those guns . . . were casted in the Washington Navy Yard under the instructions of Lieutenant J. A. Dahlgren." This bill, which President Pierce will sign into law on May 30, subverts the Missouri Compromise of 1820, for it allows slavery to exist in the territories of Kansas and Nebraska if residents want it. Pro-slavery activists cheer the law. People opposed to the expansion of slavery hate it.

JUNE 14, 1854: "There is not a shanty within a hundred miles of this city which is such a complete tinder-box as is this Capitol," declares Pennsylvania representative Joseph Chandler in the House Chamber. Claiming that the dome "invites fire," Chandler adds, "There is a nest of dry materials there covered over with tarred paper, that seems almost to threaten conflagration without the use of the torch—a spontaneous combustion." Congress soon approves the construction of a new cast-iron dome for the Capitol.

FEBRUARY 6, 1857: The National Theatre burns down. Again.

MARCH 4, 1857: The inauguration of the fifteenth U.S. president, James Buchanan, a Pennsylvanian and no slaveholder. "It snowed a little and rained a little."

MARCH 6, 1857: The U.S. Supreme Court delivers its ruling in the Dred Scott case. The court rules against a black couple, Dred and Harriet Scott, who are seeking freedom on the grounds that they have at times been in captivity on free soil. The high court also declares that the federal government can't ban slavery in the nation's territories. Chief Justice Roger Taney, Francis Scott Key's brother-in-law, declares that blacks are not, and cannot ever be, citizens.

JUNE 1, 1857: A white street gang out of Baltimore—the Plug Uglies—in league with the anti-foreigner Know-Nothing Party, disrupts local elections in the capital, aiming to swing them in favor of Know-Nothing candidates. At the polls, Plug Uglies shoot, club, and throw stones and bricks at people. The Marines are called in, "and one of the Marines [is] shot in the face and severely wounded."

FEBRUARY 6, 1858: Fighting breaks out in the Capitol's House Chamber after an anti-slavery member from Pennsylvania, Galusha Grow, and a pro-slavery member from South Carolina, Laurence Keitt, hurl insults at each other, then blows. About fifty lawmakers take part in the brawl. This happens during a late-night-into-morning session on whether to admit Kansas as a slave state. When Kansas enters the Union in January 1861, it will do so as a free state.

OCTOBER 16, 1859: "The people of Harper's Ferry, Va., was highly excited by the appearance of an individual called Captain John Osawatomie Brown." Hoping to spark a great uprising against slavery, the intrepid fifty-nine-year-old white abolitionist John Brown and his band of black and white men had attacked the federal arsenal at Harpers Ferry to steal weapons.

OCTOBER 17, 1859: "And the honorable James Buchanan, President of the United States, and the honorable Isaac Toucey, secretary of the Navy, sent orders down to Colonel John Howard, commanding officer of the Marine Corps at Washington, for all Marines that was active for to dispatch off to Harpers Ferry." Several of the raiders were killed. Others, like Brown, were later tried for treason, among other charges, then hanged.

MARCH 4, 1861: The inauguration of the sixteenth U.S. president, Abraham Lincoln. This Kentucky-born former Illinois representative was never a slaveholder.

APRIL 12, 1861: The Civil War begins when Southerners in rebellion against the United States fire on Fort Sumter in Charleston Harbor, South Carolina.

APRIL 16, 1862: Slavery is abolished in the District of Columbia. "And thanks be to the Almighty!"

SEPTEMBER 22, 1862: President Lincoln issues the preliminary Emancipation Proclamation. He announces that on New Year's Day 1863 he will declare free every person enslaved in rebel-held territory, about three million people. Part of this proclamation will be copied down in Shiner's book.

JANUARY 1, 1863: President Lincoln issues the Emancipation Proclamation because the Confederacy has not ceased and desisted from rebellion by this date. In addition to declaring free people enslaved in designated places, the proclamation states that black men can join the Union Army.

DECEMBER 2, 1863: The installation of the Statue of Freedom atop the Capitol's new dome is completed. Philip Reid, an enslaved master craftsman, played a pivotal role in the casting of this bronze statue, which weighs about 15,000 pounds and stands nearly twenty feet tall. When the Statue of Freedom is installed, Reid is a free man. The entire dome, now complete, will become the best-known symbol of American democracy; it has used up more than eight million pounds of cast iron and cost about $1 million.

APRIL 15, 1865: A few hours after Lincoln's death, Vice President Andrew Johnson, a former Tennessee slaveholder, is sworn in as the seventeenth U.S.

president. Location: Kirkwood House, a hotel on the corner of Pennsylvania Avenue and Twelfth Street NW, where Johnson has been living.

DECEMBER 6, 1865: The Thirteenth Amendment, abolishing slavery in the United States, is ratified by the necessary three-fourths of the states. It will become part of the Constitution on December 18.

1867: Michael Shiner buys 8,792 square feet of land. People call it "Shiner's Lake," "Shiner's Pond," and "Lake Shiner" because much of it is a skating pond. After draining and filling it, Shiner builds a home on this property. It is worth $4,000 by the summer of 1870. Its eventual address: 338 Ninth Street SE.

JANUARY 13, 1869: Day one of the National Convention of Colored Men in Union League Hall. The goal: to make loud and clear the black desire for voting rights and equality under the law. At the time, Congress is debating the Fifteenth Amendment, through which black men would gain the right to vote in both state and federal elections.

MARCH 4, 1869: The inauguration of the eighteenth U.S. president, Ulysses S. Grant, a Union war hero and Ohio native who briefly held one person in slavery (he freed him in 1859). "And it rained up till twelve o'clock but not hard and there it held up raining but yet was cloudy."

MARCH 31, 1869: In its report on the Sixth Ward Republican Club's weekly meeting, the *Evening Star* writes, "Michael Shiner said prompt action should be taken while Congress was here, as the Secretary of the Navy was controlled by Admiral Porter. A member here stated that Admiral Porter, in charge of the yard, was opposed to employing darkies or their white friends."

DECEMBER 31, 1870: The federal district has nearly 132,000 inhabitants. A little over 88,000 are white, and a little over 43,000 are black. The 1870 census records fifteen people who would fall under today's category of "American Indian, Eskimo, and Aleut" and three under "Asian and Pacific Islander."

Magnificent thoroughfares, for which Washington has no rival, have been lately graded, paved, and parked, and richly adorned on either side with beautiful and flourishing shade trees. The Capitol grounds, . . . formerly a picture of neglect and ugliness, have been . . . clothed with the entrancing power of landscape beauty.

Splendid mansions of every variety of modern architecture have been erected in all parts of the city. . . .

The magnificent distances of old have been mastered by street railways. . . . I often reflect that an American citizen cannot do a better thing for himself or for his country than to visit Washington at least once. . . .

Washington should loom before our mental vision, not merely as an assemblage of magnificent public buildings and a profusion of fine and fashionable people; not merely as the seat of national power and greatness; not merely as the fortunate place where the nation's great men assemble from year to year to shape the policy, enact the laws, and control the destiny of the Republic. . . . We should contemplate it with much the same feeling with which we contemplate . . . the Star-Spangled Banner, . . . a glorious symbol of civil and religious liberty. . . .

No longer sandwiched between two slave states; no longer a standing contradiction to the spirit of progress and to the civilization of the age . . . Washington may not only become one of the most beautiful and attractive cities in the world, but one of the grandest agents in the work of spreading peace on earth and good will toward men.

—Frederick Douglass, from "A Lecture on Our National Capital"

An optimistic Douglass delivered this speech on May 8, 1877, in Baltimore, where he had worked as a caulker at a shipyard for a time. After Douglass escaped slavery in 1838 by posing as a free sailor, he lived in the Northeast. In 1877, he moved to Washington D. C.

★ AUTHOR'S NOTE ★

I was at work on another book when I stumbled upon two pages from *Michael Shiner His Book* on the Library of Congress's website. I puzzled over the scrawl, the lack of punctuation, the misspellings ("wensday" for "Wednesday," "wher" for "were" and for "was"). But I was hooked. These pages told of the harrowing days when Shiner feared he'd lost his wife and children for good. I wanted to know more.

I soon discovered online John G. Sharp's transcription of Shiner's book. The more I read, the more I was in awe and astonishment. Michael Shiner, who spent many years as an Ordinary man, was anything but. He had a magic to him. A luck. And what pluck!

I include in this his bold desire to leave behind a chronicle of his life and times. That's not something workaday people usually do, preoccupied as they are with shelter, food, and other basics—and often believing that committing memories to paper is something only the Very Important People ought to do. Shiner, a true American original, knew better. He also had the gumption to reveal some of his foibles and failings and didn't feel compelled to present himself only in a positive light. In writing his book, he seems to have had no other agenda than to remember. One can't help but think that behind it was a desire to be remembered.

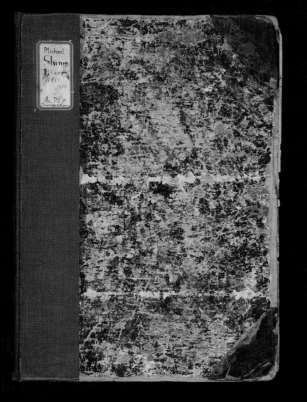

The cover and page fifty-two of *Michael Shiner His Book*. Most of the book is written in this hand. Dozens of pages are in more refined hands. It is possible that these pages were recopied by or dictated to members of Shiner's family.

Mary Ann Shiner Almarolia, from the *Washington Times*, September 5, 1904. Mary Ann seems to have inherited her father's temperament; perhaps she inherited his looks as well.

Given that so many of Shiner's memories are of major moments in the history of Washington, D.C., my editor and I felt it was only natural to tell of the capital's early days along with Shiner's story. After all, he did watch the capital grow up.

In my effort to bring Shiner's memories to a wider audience, I offer a translation of his words, as opposed to a transcription. In quoting from his book, I've silently corrected his grammar and spelling in such a way as to make him readable and yet to retain his voice. I did not want to make him appear more learned than he was. All we know about his education comes from an 1860s report on D.C. schools that singled out Michael Shiner as one of the people who took advantage of classes for blacks held at the First Presbyterian Church starting sometime in 1826. We don't know whether Shiner attended classes with or without his owner's permission. Nor do we know how long he attended. What's more, John G. Sharp believes it likely that Shiner took lessons at the impromptu school under a huge tree at the Yard run by white itinerant teacher Thomas Tabb. And it's tempting to imagine Shiner, over the years, honing his skills in private, at night by candlelight. However, several federal censuses present Shiner as someone who could neither read nor write. Did census takers make mistakes or make assumptions? Did Michael Shiner feel that it was best if he kept his bit of literacy to himself for a time?

Unknowns about Shiner abound, from the identity of his parents and exactly how many children he had to precisely when he gained his freedom. Often I had no choice but to make informed, educated guesses, recognizing that when it comes to history, there's so much we do not know. Whereas it was once commonplace to present supposition as fact and even to make things up (George Washington and the cherry tree, for example), over the years more writers have come to understand that there is no shame in saying, "I don't know." Just about every book of history is a work in progress. We never know when a diary or document will be found up in an attic or beneath worn floorboards—material that gives us new information, new answers, and new challenges to what we thought we knew.

With Michael Shiner, the most bedeviling unknown is what he looked like. I found no engraving or photograph of the man. Was he short and stocky? Tall and thin? Was he ebony, mahogany, caramel, cream?

One solace was finding a photograph of his daughter Mary Ann, the keeper of his book and his historical memorabilia. When her father died, thirty-eight-year-old Mary Ann was living at 116 Maryland Avenue SW. In her household were her three-year-old son, Lewis; ten-year-old daughter, Lottie; and husband, Alexander Almarolia, a sixty-two-year-old Italian immigrant who ran a dining saloon on Maryland Avenue. (Mary Ann's husband died nine months after Michael Shiner, in October 1880.) Mary Ann, who sometimes used the surname Alexander (because Almarolia was hard for people to pronounce), stayed in the restaurant business for a while.

Like her father, Mary Ann was a very bold soul. She married a white man at a time when interracial marriages were far more controversial than they are today (and black-and-white marriages were illegal in many states). Too, she got into some scrapes and even ran afoul of the law, but according to one article—in which she again is made to sound like her father—"some very prominent men" in Washington helped get her out of trouble. After Mary Ann died, in 1904, newspapers buzzed with stories about her estate and about her son, Lewis, not being her biological child and really being white, like another "son," Joseph. But that's another story.

As for Shiner's book, it was Lewis who apparently became its guardian. Using the surname Alexander, he sold it to the Library of Congress in 1906 for $10 (equivalent to about $250 today).

I can hear Michael Shiner shouting, as he did about the end of slavery in D.C., "And thanks be to the Almighty!" Not about the money his book fetched but about its assured preservation and the prospect that he, Michael Shiner, would be remembered.

"I, Michael Shiner have seen eleven presidents take their seats and some of those presidents I have seen take their seats twice." These words are from the last entry in Shiner's book, in which he recollected Inauguration Day, 1869.

GLOSSARY

Definitions of words and phrases are given relative to their use in this book.

abolitionist: someone who worked for the immediate end of slavery in America.

black codes: laws passed before and after the Civil War to control black people. Some of these regulations also controlled white people, for example by fining and/or imprisoning them for associating with black people.

boatswain (pronounced "bo-sun"): a senior crewman responsible for the sails, anchors, and others aspects of the deck of a ship.

camboose: a stove often located on the deck. Also, a ship's galley.

capital: the seat of a government. Also, an adjective meaning "excellent" or "splendid."

capitol: a building in which a body of lawmakers meets.

Capitol: the building in which the U.S. Congress meets.

caulker: a person who makes ships and boats watertight. In the nineteenth century, the process involved filling cracks with jute or hemp, then sealing them with tar.

coffle: a group of animals or people chained or otherwise fastened together in a line.

Congreve rocket: a weapon developed by the Englishman Sir William Congreve in the early 1800s. Congreve rockets were more accurate and had a longer range (about three miles) than the rockets previously in use (which had a range of about a mile). Congreve based his rocket design on one developed in India.

cooper: a maker or repairer of the wooden staves of a ship's hull, and of casks and barrels.

cornerstone: the foundational stone of a building.

coxswain (pronounced "kok-sun"): a person in charge of a small boat, such as a lifeboat, and its crew.

cut up shines: to play tricks or pranks, to act out.

emancipate: to liberate.

flagship: the ship that carries a fleet's commander.

frigate: a warship.

gig: a boat reserved for the use of a ship's captain.

grog shop: a saloon or bar that usually sold cheap alcoholic drinks. "Grog" originally referred to a drink of watered-down rum given to British sailors because freshwater aboard vessels didn't stay fresh very long.

gunwale (pronounced "gun–nel"): the upper edge of the side of a ship or boat.

jolly boat: a small boat usually stored aboard a ship and used for errands, such as transporting people or supplies to and from shore or another ship.

manumit: to set free.

pilot bread: a type of biscuit, also known as hardtack.

privateer: private person (or that person's ship) commissioned by his or her government during wartime to attack and plunder enemy vessels for a percentage of the loot.

rigger: a person in charge of the ropes and chains used to support and work different parts of a sailing vessel, such as its masts and sails.

sloop of war: for most of the nineteenth century, a warship with fewer than twenty guns.

Stars and Stripes: the national flag of the United States, also known as the Star-Spangled Banner or Old Glory.

Union Jack: the national flag of the United Kingdom, officially called the Union Flag.

NOTES

If not cited below, all information about Michael Shiner and the people in his life, as well as quotations by Shiner and others, is from his book. John G. Sharp's annotated transcription, with an introduction, is available online from the Navy Department Library under the title *The Diary of Michael Shiner Relating to the History of the Washington Navy Yard 1813–1869.*

Population figures for the District of Columbia are based on the U.S. Census Bureau's Table 23, "District of Columbia—Race and Hispanic Origin: 1800 to 1990" (PDF; Internet release date: September 13, 2002).

Full citations for major works consulted can be found in Selected Sources.

page vi "A cluster of houses at the Navy Yard": Byron Sunderland, *A Sketch of the Life of Dr. William Gunton, Born at Aylsham, Norfolk, England, October 29th, 1791* (Washington, D.C.: Joseph L. Pearson, 1878), 14–15.

Chapter 1 "Flames of Fire" and "Rockets' Red Glare"

page 3 Shiner's year of birth: Certificate of Death #22895. District of Columbia Archives.

page 4 Robert Sewall's house: Sewall at one time rented the house to Treasury Secretary Albert Gallatin. On the site now stands the Sewall-Belmont House Museum (144 Constitution Avenue NE).

page 7 "the most splendid and beautiful city": Jefferson Morley, *Snow-Storm in August*, 14.

page 8 "To a Bostonian or a Philadelphian": Richard Rush to John Adams, September 5, 1814. Historical Society of Pennsylvania.

page 9 "We have agreed that the Federal District": *Records of the Columbia Historical Society*, vol. 2 (Washington, D.C.: Columbia Historical Society, 1899), 131–32.

page 10 "such books as may be necessary": *The Public Statutes at Large of the United States of America, from the Organization of the Government in 1789, to March*

1845, vol. 2 (Boston: Charles C. Little and James Brown, 1845), 56.

page 10 President Jefferson notified of the arrival of books: Thomas Mann, Humanities and Social Sciences Division, Library of Congress, e-mail to author, August 14, 2013.

page 11 "James Smith, a free colored man": Paul Jennings, *A Colored Man's Reminiscences of James Madison*, 8–11.

Chapter 2 Hard Winters, an Apple Tree, and Freedom on His Mind

page 12 "I confess that I was so unfeminine": Allen C. Clark, *Life and Letters of Dolly Madison* (Washington, D.C.: Press of W. F. Roberts Company, 1914), 166–67.

page 16 Shiner at the Yard as a teen: As John G. Sharp notes in "African Americans in Slavery and Freedom on the Washington Navy Yard," Shiner's first mention of the Yard is in his entry for 1819, when he was about fourteen. The entry is about the construction of the USS *Columbus*, a seventy-four-gun ship of the line.

page 16 Shiner's date of purchase and purchase price: Recounting events of January 29, 1829, Shiner wrote, "And I had jest belong to Mr. Howard Sr. one year that day." However, "A List of Property Belonging to the Estate of William Pumphrey, Deceased, Sold by His

Executors at Private Sale in Pursuance of an Order of the Orphans Court," which gives Shiner's purchase price as $250, is dated September 8, 1828. This document was provided by John G. Sharp. His citation: Maryland State Archives Prince Georges County Register of Wills (Inventories) 1817–1829 C1228 William Pumphrey (Slaveholder) Liber TT 7 Folio 218.

page 16 Thomas Howard's address: *The Washington Directory*, 1827 (Washington D.C.: S. A. Elliott), 42.

page 17 "blocks, chain cables": Sharp, "Note to Navy Yard 1861 Illustration for Tonya Bolden," November 27, 2013.

page 17 work of "Ordinary" men: "Washington Navy Yard Station Log Nov. 1822–Mar. 1830 Extracts."

page 17 weather on July 4, 1828: "Washington Navy Yard Station Log."

page 17 Yard labor force in 1808 and 1830: John G. Sharp, "African Americans in Slavery and Freedom on the Washington Navy Yard," 8, and John G. Sharp e-mail to author, July 21, 2014.

page 18 "It happened that": John Quincy Adams diary 36, 1 January 1825–30 September 1830, 20, in *The Diaries of John Quincy Adams: A Digital Collection* (Boston: Massachusetts Historical Society, 2004). http://www.masshist.org/jqadiaries.

page 18 George Lee: David Watterston purchased George Lee (then about twenty-four) in November 1810 from Richard Bullock of Washington, D.C., for $400 (Helen Hoban Rogers, compiler, *Freedom & Slavery Documents in the District of Columbia*, vol. 2, 124). In his will, Watterston mandated that two black men, George and Moses, be freed "after the day of [his] decease" and that all his "wearing apparel" go to "negro man George" ("Internments in the Historic Congressional Cemetery," PDF, http://www.congressionalcemetery.org/sites/defaults/files/Obits_Watterston.pdf).

page 19 "If her tongue": "Notice," advertisement in *Daily National Intelligencer*, August 11, 1821, 1.

page 20 "often acted for . . . a job": John G. Sharp, e-mail to author, February 6, 2013.

page 20 "one could easily get drunk": Jefferson Morley, *Snow-Storm in August*, 16.

page 20 the Jarvis–Adams affair: Samuel Flagg Bemis, "The Scuffle in the Rotunda: A Footnote to the Presidency of John Quincy Adams and to the History of Dueling," in *Proceedings of the Massachusetts Historical Society*, 3rd series, vol. 71 (Oct. 1953–May 1957), 156–66.

page 20 on the justice of the peace: Shiner gave the man's name as "Clemont Huit." I found no one with that name, but in December 1828 John Quincy Adams nominated a William Hewitt of the District of Columbia to serve as a justice of the peace until March 1829 (*Journal of the Executive Proceedings of the Senate of the United States of America*, vol. 3, [Washington, D.C.: Duff Green, 1828], 620–21).

page 21 ear cropping: Worthington G. Snethen, *The Black Code of the District of Columbia, in Force September 1st, 1848,* 14.

page 21 the pass system: John G. Sharp, e-mail to author, February 20, 2013.

page 22 "One day I went to see the 'slaves' pen' ": E. S. Abdy, *Journal of a Residence and Tour in the United States of North America, from April, 1833, to October, 1834,* vol. 2 (London: John Murray, 1835), 96–97.

page 22 log entry: "Remarks & Occurrences in the Navy Yard Washington: Thomas Tingey, Esq. Commander," December 24–January 2, 1829. Provided by John G. Sharp. His citation: National Archives and Records Administration, Record Group 181.14, Records of the Washington Navy Yard (Washington, D.C.), Station Log Nov. 1822–Mar. 1830.

page 26 William Pumphrey Jr.'s will: Will of William Pumphrey, Prince Georges County, MD, Liber TT 1 Folio 423, in Edythe Maxey Clark, *William Pumphrey of Prince George's County, Maryland, and His Descendants*, 10.

page 26 Thomas Howard's will: Will of Thomas Howard, District of Columbia Archives, and

"Obituary—Howard, Thomas," Association for the Preservation of the Historic Congressional Cemetery, http://www.congressionalcemetery.org/obituary-howard-thomas.

page 27 certificate for Phillis [Shiner]: Provided by John G. Sharp. His citation: District of Columbia Archives, Recorder of Deeds, James Pumphrey, slave certificate for: "Phillis" Liber AP No. 40, dated 9 October 1817, 28.

page 28 Thomas Howard and James Pumphrey in Ward Five: 1820 United States Federal Census (online database). Accessed at Ancestry.com.

page 28 James Pumphrey's property up for sale and purchase price of $295: "Sale, Under an Order of the Orphan's Court of the Personal Effects of James Pumphrey Deceased April 27th 1832." Provided by John G. Sharp. His citation: James Pumphrey's Probate File. National Archives and Records Administration RG21 Entry 115, 0.5 Case File 1569.

page 30 manumission of Phillis Shiner and children: Page from record book provided by John G. Sharp. His citation: National Archives and Records Administration, Record Group 21, Records of the District Courts of the United States, District of Columbia, Entry 30, Manumission and Emancipation, 1821–62, Levi Pumphrey to Phillis Shiner, June 13, 1833.

page 30 Levi Pumphrey's ad: *Daily National Intelligencer*, September 28, 1858, 1.

page 31 "a perfect savage": William Still, *The Underground Railroad: A Record of Facts, Authentic Narratives, Letters, &c.* (Philadelphia: Porter & Coates, 1872), 480.

page 32 "many men and women": M. B. Goodwin, "Schools and Education of the Colored Population in the District," Appendix C in S*pecial Report of the Commissioner of Education on the Condition and Improvement of Public Schools in the District of Columbia* (Washington, D.C.: Government Printing Office, 1871), 221.

Chapter 3 An Ax, a "Snow-Storm," Lunch Baskets, and Brickbats

page 34 "Two weeks have passed since we located ourselves": Gaillard Hunt, ed., *The First Forty Years of Washington Society*, 238–41.

page 37 goods: "Earthenware, China & Glass," "New Books," and "Valuable Medicines," advertisements in *Daily National Intelligencer*, November 2, 1833, 1.

page 37 "We will at all times pay higher prices": "Cash for Negroes," advertisement in *Daily National Intelligencer*, November 2, 1833, 1.

page 37 "About five feet ten inches high": "$100 Reward," advertisement in *Daily National Intelligencer*, October 11, 1833, 1.

page 38 horse theft: "Stop Thief," advertisement in *Daily National Intelligencer*, June 22, 1833, 1.

page 38 robbery of store: "Twenty Dollars Reward," advertisement in *Daily National Intelligencer*, July 16, 1833, 3.

page 40 "I'll have my freedom, you hear me?": Morley, *Snow-Storm in August*, 126.

page 40 "The first fruit": *Daily National Intelligencer*, August 7, 1835, 3.

page 41 "first true restaurants": Morley, *Snow-Storm in August,* 34.

page 41 "marched into his schoolhouse": Goodwin, "Schools and Education of the Colored Population," 201.

page 41 "Parents, guardians, and others": *Daily National Intelligencer*, August 13, 1835, 1.

page 43 Isaac Hull's order: John G. Sharp, "Race and Labor," 15.

page 46 Snow's claim of innocence: "To the Editors," *Daily National Intelligencer*, August 27, 1835, 3.

page 47 on suits for freedom: Among the best-known is Elizabeth Freeman, a great-grandmother of the scholar-activist W.E.B. DuBois. Freeman was one of the first blacks in Massachusetts to successfully sue for freedom. She did so in 1781. As for precedents in Washington, D.C., as John G. Sharp points out: "Shiner and the African American community actively followed the news, and as a former slave of the Pumphrey family knew well of three important petitions for freedom. These are: *Negro Charlotte v John Pumphrey*, April Term 1823, *Negro Leanna & Child v Lloyd Pumphrey* and *Negro Rebecca and Children v Lloyd Pumphrey*, Dec Term 1824." April 11, 2014, e-mail to author from John G. Sharp when providing documents pertaining to Shiner's petition for freedom. He learned of their existence from Leslie Anderson's Overbeck History Lecture on Michael Shiner.

page 47 Shiner in 1840 census: Sixth U.S. Census, 1840. Accessed at Ancestry.com.

page 48 "Am I gagged or am I not?": Harlow Giles Unger, *John Quincy Adams*, 274.

page 48 "Gag rule": *Journal of the House of Representatives of the United States*, vol. 29. (Washington: printed by Blair and Rives, 1836), 882.

page 48 "But I take higher ground": Richard K. Craillé, ed., *Speeches of John C. Calhoun* (New York: D. Appleton, 1860), 631–32.

page 49 anti-slavery petitions to Congress: Leonard L. Richards, *The Slave Power*, 136.

page 49 "Again and again I asserted": Solomon Northup, *Twelve Years a Slave* (London: Sampson Low, Son & Co., 1853), 43.

Chapter 4 A "Singular Mark," a "Splendid Day," and Standing by the Stars and Stripes

page 50 "It is sometimes called the City of Magnificent Distances": Charles Dickens, *American Notes for General Circulation*, 2nd ed., vol. 1 (London: Chapman and Hall, 1842): 281–84.

page 53 black codes: Worthington G. Snethen, *The Black Code of the District of Columbia*, 30 (idleness), 40 (get-togethers), 45 (licenses), 45–46 (taverns and eateries).

page 53 Shiner's pay: John G. Sharp, "History of the Washington Navy Yard Civilian Workforce, 1799–1962," 94. Here one finds a page from the 1845 Washington Navy Yard book with Michael Shiner listed among the painters' helpers. All made $2.25 a day.

page 54 *Princeton* explosion: Lee M. Pearson, "The *Princeton* and the Peacemaker: A Study in Nineteenth-Century Naval Research and Development Procedures," *Technology and Culture*, vol. 7, no. 2 (Spring 1966), 163–83; and Ann Blackman, "Fatal Cruise of the *Princeton*," *Naval History* (September 2005), accessed at http://military.com.

page 55 "Upon turning my eyes towards [the Peacemaker]": St. George L. Sioussat, ed., "The Accident On Board the USS *Princeton*, February 28, 1844: A Contemporary Newsletter," *Pennsylvania History*, July 1937, 176–77.

page 55 Shiner's conversation with an acquaintance: Shiner wrote that he was speaking with Gustavas Higdon. A man by that name was the owner of dry goods store that, as John G. Sharp has noted, "did a lot business with the Washington Navy" (*The Diary of Michael Shiner*, n. 62). However, Gustavas Higdon died in 1838 (*Daily National Intelligencer*, June 27, 1838). Who Shiner meant is unknown.

page 55 "whose skull and head were shattered": "Local News," *Daily National Intelligencer*, February 13, 1846, 4.

page 56 "sacrificed half a day's pay": "City News," *Daily National Intelligencer*, June 9, 1848, 1.

page 56 report on fire: "National Calamity," *National Era*, January 1, 1852, 4.

page 57 Shiner's marriage to Jane Jackson: On September 8, 1849. Historical court records of Washington, District of Columbia (online database). Accessed at Ancestry.com.

page 57 Shiners in 1850 census: Seventh U.S. Census. Accessed at Ancestry.com.

page 57 Jane widowed: "Lawsuit Her Bequest," *Washington Post*, September 1, 1904, 5. According to this article, Jane had a daughter named Jennie from her first marriage.

page 58 "We ask you to join us": Robert Barnwell Rhett, *The Address of the People of South Carolina, Assembled in Convention, to the People of the Slaveholding States of the United States* (Charleston, S.C.: Evans & Cogswell, 1860), 6.

page 63 Shiner contracted to do construction work: "Board of Public Works," *The Critic*, September 26, 1871, 3.

page 63 Shiner as marshal's aide and watchman: *Evening Star*, November 10, 1869, 4, col. 1; and "The Police Board," *National Republican*, November 19, 1875. Also, Shiner's death certificate states that he was a watchman when he died.

page 64 Shiner's death: Certificate of Death #22895. District of Columbia Archives. Though it states that Shiner died on January 16, 1880, it also states that he was buried on January 17, 1880.

page 64 Shiner in the *Evening Star*: "Not a Case of Small-Pox Per Day," *Evening Star*, January 17, 1880, 8; and "The Death of Uncle Mike Shiner," *Evening Star*, January 19, 1880, 1.

page 64 Shiner's memorabilia: "Man About Town," *Washington Post*, October 3, 1892, 5.

page 69 Act ending slave trade in Washington, D.C.: George Minot, ed., *Statutes at Large and Treaties of the United States of America from December 1, 1845, to March 3, 1851* (Boston: Little, Brown, 1862), 467–68.

page 69 "Ran away from Subscriber": Advertisement in *Daily National Intelligencer*, April 12, 1853, 3.

page 69 "There is not a shanty . . . combustion": William C. Allen, *History of the United States Capitol*, 225.

page 71 Shiner's acquisition of property in 1867: "Holtzman v. Linton," in *Reports of Cases Adjudged in the Court of Appeals of the District of Columbia from February 6, 1906 to June 5, 1906* (New York: Lawyers Co-operative, 1906), 248.

page 71 "Michael Shiner said prompt action should be taken": "Local News," *Evening Star*, March 31, 1869, 4.

Author's Note

page 72 "Magnificent thoroughfares, for which Washington has no rival": *Frederick Douglass: A Lecture on Our National Capital* (Washington, D.C.: Smithsonian Institution Press, 1978), 13–44.

page 75 on Mary Ann's sons being white: "Lewis Alexander Tells His Life Story," *Washington Times*, August 21, 1904, 5; "Love, Hate, and Romance Mingle in Life of Negress Just Dead," *Washington Times*, August 28, 1904, 6; and "Almarolia Case in Statu Quo," *Washington Times*, September 5, 1904, 10.

page 75 "some very prominent men": "Revolting Depravity," *Cleveland Leader*, July 11, 1885, 2.

page 75 purchase of Shiner's book: Dr. Adrienne Cannon, manuscript specialist, Library of Congress, e-mail to author, February 7, 2013.

SELECTED SOURCES

Allen, William C. *History of the United States Capitol: A Chronicle of Design, Construction, and Politics.* Washington, D.C.: U.S. Government Printing Office, 2001.

Anderson, Leslie. "Who Was Michael Shiner?" Overbeck History Lecture at the Naval Lodge Hall, Washington, D.C., February 4, 2014. Telecast on C-Span, March 1, 2014, under the title "Life of Freed Slave Michael Shiner."

Brown, Gordon S. *The Captain Who Burned His Ships: Captain Thomas Tingey, USN, 1750–1829.* Annapolis, Md.: Naval Institute Press, 2011.

Brown, Letitia Woods. *Free Negroes in the District of Columbia, 1790–1846:* New York: Oxford University Press, 1972.

Clark, Edythe Maxey. *William Pumphrey of Prince George's County, Maryland, and His Descendants.* Decorah, Iowa: Anundsen, 1992. http://usgwarchives.net/md/statewide/ClarkCollection/pumphrey/.

Fitzpatrick, Sandra, and Maria R. Goodwin. *The Guide to Black Washington: Places and Events of Historical and Cultural Significance in the Nation's Capital.* Rev. illustrated ed. New York: Hippocrene Books, 2001.

Gutheim, Frederick, and Antoinette J. Lee. *Worthy of the Nation:* Washington, DC, from *L'Enfant to the National Capital Planning Committee.* 2nd ed. Baltimore: Johns Hopkins University Press, 2006.

Harrold, Stanley. Subversives: *Antislavery Community in Washington, D.C., 1828–1865.* Baton Rouge: Louisiana State University Press, 2003.

Hibben, Henry B. *Navy-Yard, Washington: History from Organization, 1799 to Present Date.* Washington, D.C.: Government Printing Office, 1890.

Hickey, Donald R. *The War of 1812: A Forgotten Conflict.* Bicentennial ed. Urbana: University of Illinois Press, 2012.

Holland, Jesse J. *Black Men Built the Capitol: Discovering African-American History in and Around Washington, D.C.* Guilford, Conn.: Globe Pequot, 2007. Kindle edition.

Hunt, Gaillard, ed. *The First Forty Years of Washington Society.* New York: C. Scribner's Sons, 1906.

Jennings, Paul. *A Colored Man's Reminiscences of James Madison.* Brooklyn, N.Y.: G. C. Beadle, 1865.

Marolda, Edward J. *The Washington Navy Yard: An Illustrated History.* Honolulu, Hawaii: University Press of the Pacific, 2004. First published 1999 by Naval Historical Center.

Meacham, Jon. *American Lion: Andrew Jackson in the White House.* New York: Random House, 2008.

Morley, Jefferson. *Snow-Storm in August: Washington City, Francis Scott Key, and the Forgotten Race Riot of 1835.* New York: Nan A. Talese/Doubleday, 2012. Kindle edition.

Passonneau, Joseph R. *Washington Through Two Centuries: A History in Maps and Images.* New York: Monacelli, 2004.

Pitch, Anthony S. *The Burning of Washington: The British Invasion of 1814.* Annapolis, Md.: Bluejacket Books/Naval Institute Press, 2000. First published 1998 by Naval Institute Press.

"Remarks & Occurrences in the Navy Yard Washington: Thomas Tingey, Esq. Commander," December 24–January 2, 1829. Photographed by John G. Sharp. JPG e-mailed to author February 5, 2013.

Richards, Leonard L. *The Slave Power: The Free North and Southern Dominion, 1780–1860.* Baton Rouge: Louisiana State University Press, 2000.

Ricks, Mary Kay. *Escape on the* Pearl: *The Heroic Bid for Freedom on the Underground Railroad.* New York: HarperCollins, 2009. Kindle edition. First published 2007 by William Morrow.

Rogers, Helen Hoban, compiler. *Freedom & Slavery Documents in the District of Columbia, v*ols. 1–3. Baltimore: Gateway, 2007, 2008, 2009.

Seale, William. *The President's House: A History*, vols. 1 & 2, 2nd edition. Washington, D.C.: White House Historical Association, 2008.

Sharp, John G. "African Americans in Slavery and Freedom on the Washington Navy Yard, 1799–1865." Unpublished manuscript e-mailed to author January 23, 2013.

——, transcriber. *The Diary of Michael Shiner Relating to the History of the Washington Navy Yard 1813–1869.* http://www.history.navy.mil/library/online/shinerdiary .htm

——. *History of the Washington Navy Yard Civilian Workforce, 1799–1962.* PDF. www.history.navy.mil/books/ sharp/WNY_History.pdf.

——. "Note to Navy Yard 1861 Illustration for Tonya Bolden." Unpublished manuscript e-mailed to author November 27, 2013.

——. "Race and Labor: The Washington Navy Yard Strike and 'Snow Riot' of 1835." Unpublished manuscript e-mailed to author February 22, 2013.

——, transcriber. "Washington Navy Yard Station Log Nov. 1822–Mar. 1830 Extracts." Revised March 18, 2012. Unpublished manuscript e-mailed to author February 5, 2013.

Shiner, Michael. *The Diary of Michael Shiner: Relating to the History of the Washington Navy Yard, 1813–1869.* Transcribed by John G. Sharp. Washington, D.C.: Navy Department Library, 2007.

Snethen, Worthington G. *The Black Code of the District of Columbia, in Force September 1st, 1848.* New York: William Harned, 1848.

Tremain, Mary. *Slavery in the District of Columbia: The Policy of Congress and the Struggle for Abolition.* New York: G. P. Putnam's Sons, 1892.

Unger, Harlow Giles. *John Quincy Adams.* Boston: Da Capo, 2012.

ACKNOWLEDGMENTS

John G. Sharp: This book is because you were. I am forever grateful for your years of painstaking research and work on Michael Shiner and his book; for your extraordinary generosity in sharing so many documents, so many insights; and for your willingness to read drafts and layouts. Thanks are also due John's lovely wife, Gene, another Shiner researcher and connoisseur.

This book also benefited from the kindnesses of many strangers. At Belmont Mansion: Mark Brown, director. At the District of Columbia Archives: Ali Rahmaan, archivist, and Danny Brown, staff assistant. At the Historical Society of Pennsylvania: Steven Smith, public service librarian. At the Huntington Library: Lita Garcia, library associate; Olga Tsapina Norris Foundation Curator, American Historical Manuscripts; and James Glisson, Bradford and Christine Mishler assistant curator of American Art. At James Madison's Montpelier: Tiffany W. Cole, assistant curator of research. At the James Monroe Museum and Memorial Library: Scott Harris, director. At the Library of Congress: Adrienne Cannon, manuscript specialist; Bonnie B. Coles, senior information and reference specialist; and Thomas Mann, reference librarian. At the Moorland-Spingarn Research Center, Howard University: Kenvi Phillips, prints and photographs librarian. At the National Archives and Records Administration: Robert Ellis and Chris Killilay, archivists. At the Naval History & Heritage Command, Washington Navy Yard: Glenn Helm, director, Navy Department Library; Gale Munro, head curator, Navy Art Collection; and Jon Roscoe, archivist. At the Walters Art Museum: Jo Briggs, assistant curator, and Danielle Horetsky, curatorial division assistant.

For your feedback on the final draft, thank you, fellow writers Linda Tarrant-Ried and Connie Green.

For your ongoing moral support and deft agenting, thank you, Jennifer Lyons.

Finally, I can't say enough about my colleagues at Abrams, people I so enjoy working with: my stalwart editor, Howard Reeves; editorial assistant Orlando Dos Reis (so quick!); copy editor Scott Auerbach (so adept, so discerning!); fact-checker David M. Webster (so smart!); proofreaders Richard Slovak and Kathy Brock (so eagle-eyed!); managing editor Jim Armstrong (who must have at least five brains!); associate production director Alison Gervais (who works wonders even when archival images are in rough shape!). And there's the brilliant design team of Maria Middleton, Kate Fitch, Alissa Faden, and Pamela Notarantonio, and, last but not least, the ingenious Jason Wells, executive director, publicity and marketing.

I thank you all so much for the wonderful work that you do.

IMAGE CREDITS

Case cover (front): Library of Congress. **Case cover (spine):** © National Museums Liverpool, Walker Art Gallery; author's collection. **Title page:** Library of Congress. **Page iii:** Historical Society of Washington, D.C. **Page iv:** Historical Society of Washington, D.C., Kiplinger Collection. **Page 2:** © National Museums Liverpool, Walker Art Gallery. **Page 4:** Naval History and Heritage Command. **Page 5:** Granger Collection, New York. **Page 6:** Courtesy of Maryland Historical Society, Item H89. **Page 7:** Library of Congress. **Page 8:** Library of Congress. **Page 10:** Huntington Library, San Marino, Calif. HM 52665. **Page 14:** Library of Congress. **Page 17:** Courtesy of National Archives & Records Administration, Washington, D.C. **Page 19:** Naval History and Heritage Command. **Page 23:** Library Company of Philadelphia. **Pages 24–25:** White House Historical Association and Decatur House, a National Trust Site. **Page 27:** NARA: Record Group 21, Records of the District Courts of the United States, District of Columbia, Entry 115, Old Series [Probate] Administration Case Files, 1801-78, File #1621, Thomas Howard, List of the goods belonging to the personal estate of Thomas Howard (deceased). **Page 29:** Library of Congress. **Page 30:** Library of Congress. **Page 33:** Library of Congress. **Page 36:** Library of Congress. **Page 38:** Moorland-Spingarn Research, Howard University. **Page 39:** Courtesy, National Gallery of Art, Washington. **Page 42:** Accessible Archives, Inc. **Page 43:** Library Company of Philadelphia. **Page 44:** Naval History and Heritage Command. **Page 45:** Walters Art Museum, Baltimore. **Page 46:** Courtesy of Maine Maritime Museum, Bath, Maine. **Page 47:** Record Group 21, Records of the District Courts of the United States, District of Columbia, Entry 6, Case Papers, Containing Appearances, Trials, Imparlances, Judicial, etc., 1802-63, March Term 1836, Civil Appearance #413, Michael Shiner v. A. & W. E. Howard. **Page 49:** I. N. Phelps Stokes Collection, Miriam and Ira D. Wallach Division of Art, Prints and Photographs, New York Public Library, Astor, Lenox, and Tilden Foundations. **Page 52:** Library of Congress. **Page 54:** Library of Congress. **Page 56:** Author's collection. **Page 59:** Historical Society of Washington, D.C. **Page 60:** Naval History and Heritage Command. **Page 61:** Library of Congress. **Page 62:** Library of Congress. **Page 64:** Courtesy of GeneologyBank.com, a division of NewsBank Inc. **Page 65:** Historical Society of Washington, D.C. **Page 66:** Historical Society of Washington, D.C. **Page 67:** Courtesy of the Estate of Sylvia J. Alexander and Montpelier Foundation, James Madison's Montpelier. **Page 73 (left and right):** Library of Congress. **Page 74:** Library of Congress. **Page 75:** Library of Congress.

INDEX

Note: Page numbers in *italics* refer to illustrations.

Captain William Ramsey
United States Navy the

the Monsters let me case
they who after our Handed
they couldn't catch him a
come prevailedin Alexandria
hermit that morning
rtheless the several persue
way down to Richmond les
as he who and a states
a gentleman and a Sailor
as greater one that ever
ther foot in the bilted
God allmighty above
wouldent let one arti
the fedral consatution
mple under foot if he ke
her as honest upright i
ver lived he said no Resp
hersons While ever they d

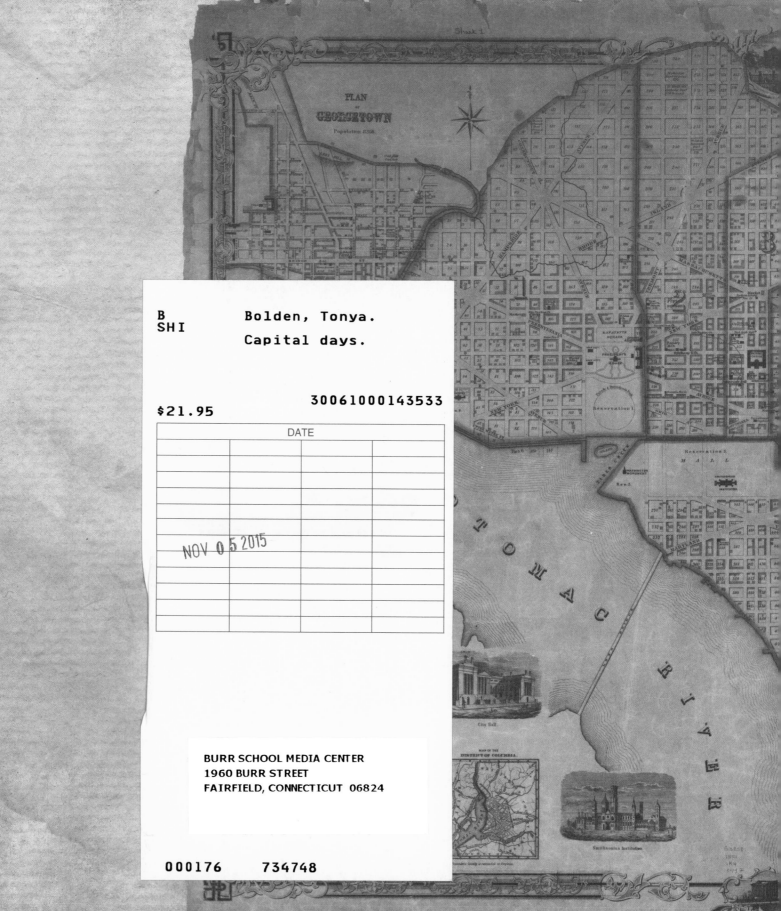

B
SHI

Bolden, Tonya.

Capital days.

$21.95

30061000143533

DATE			
NOV 0 5 2015			

000176   734748